MANAGE YOUR MICROBIOMES

Heal Your Gut, Lose Weight

Over 100 GUT friendly recipes

The Microbiome diet made easy

Vanessa Rogers

Published by ROC Publishing 2016

© This publication is copyright. Other than for purposes of and subject to the conditions prescribed in the Copyright Act, no part of it may be reproduced without prior permission. Material which is reproduced from this publication must include an acknowledgement of the source. Prior permission should be sought from the relevant office.

DISCLAIMER

The information contained herein has been posted in good faith and is to be used for educational purposes only. The author has made considerable efforts to present accurate and reliable information in this book. However, the author does not take any legal responsibility for the accuracy, completeness, or usefulness of the information herein. The information in this book is not intended to provide specific advice about individual medical or legal questions. This book should not be considered a substitute for a reader's own independent research and evaluation.

This book may contain links or refer to other web sites, and other web sites may refer to this book. Links to web sites outside of this site do not imply endorsement or approval of those sites or the information they contain. The links to other web sites are provided solely as a convenience to users of this site. The author is not responsible for the accuracy of the information, the content, or the policies of such sites, and shall not be liable for any damages or injury arising from the content or use of those sites. This content may refer to organizations, businesses, and other resources available through government, non-profit, and commercial entities. Referrals to such entities are provided solely for informational and educational purposes and as a convenience to the user. A referral to a product or service on this web site should not be considered an endorsement or recommendation of that product or service. The author shall not be liable for any damages or injury arising from the use of or connection with such products, services, or entities.

MANAGE YOUR MICROBIOMES

PART ONE: INTRODUCTION 10

What Is The Microbiome Diet? 11
It all starts in your gut! 13
Superfoods to Help With Gut Bacteria 16
Probiotic Foods 22
- The Health Benefits of Probiotics 22
- Who Should Take Probiotics? 23
- Top Probiotic Foods You Are Not Eating 23

Prebiotic Foods 39
- Meet the Prebiotics 39
- Symbiosis of Probiotics and Prebiotics 39
- Foods Rich in Prebiotics 40
- Other Health Benefits 40
- Top Prebiotic Foods 40

THE PLANT BASED DIET AND MICRO DIVERSITY 42

MICROBIOME DIET AND WEIGHT LOSS 43

Does Bad Bacteria Make You Fat? 43
Gut Bacteria and Food Cravings 45

MICROBIOME DIET FOR CERTAIN CONDITIONS 47

THE SCIENCE BEHIND THE MICROBIOME DIET 50

Your evolving microbiome 51

MAKING THE TRANSITION TO THE MICROBIOME DIET EASIER 51

PART TWO: THE MICROBIOME DIET RECIPES 56

Microbiome Breakfast Recipes 56
- Vegetable Breakfast Bakes 56
- Dill-Tomato Frittata 58
- Healthy Pumpkin Granola 59
- Healthy Breakfast Porridge 61
- Smoked Salmon and Red Pepper Scramble 62
- Broccoli and Sausage Quiche 63
- Berry Omelet 65
- Bacon & Pepper Frittata 66
- Basil Tomato Scramble 67
- Gut-Friendly Frittata 68

MANAGE YOUR MICROBIOMES

- *Berry & Cinnamon Smoothie* *70*
- *Buttermilk Kefir Herb Biscuits* *71*
- *Sausage Spinach and Cheese Strata* *73*
- *Cultured Dairy Buckwheat Pancakes* *75*
- *Salmon Egg Sandwich* *77*
- *Asparagus w/ Poached Egg* *78*
- *Coconut & Almond Pancakes W/ Spiced Plums* *81*
- *Green Smoothie* *83*
- *Amazing Veggie Frittata* *84*

MICROBIOME LUNCH RECIPES 85

- *Fennel Cucumber Salad* *85*
- *Classic Chicken Soup* *86*
- *Beer-Steamed Mussels* *87*
- *Smoked Salmon & Asparagus Bundles* *88*
- *Healthy Greek Salad W/ Sheep's Milk Feta* *89*
- *Mango Salad With Citrus Vinaigrette* *91*
- *Steamed Quinoa* *92*
- *Green Apple, Carrot & Jicama Slaw* *93*
- *Leek, Courgette and Spinach Quiche* *94*
- *Healthy Chicken Salad w/ Bread* *95*
- *Greek Tuna Bread* *96*
- **Chicken & Veggie Stew** *97*
- *Strawberry Spinach Salad* *99*
- *Chickpea Salad* *100*
- *Spinach and Beet Salad* *101*
- **Citrus and Spinach Salad** *102*
- *Avocado & Quinoa Salad* *103*
- *Cucumber & Arugula Salad W/ Lemon Dressing* *104*
- *Grapefruit-Kale Salad* *105*
- *Almond Chicken Salad* *106*
- *Healthy Curried Shrimp* *107*

MICROBIOME DIET DINNER RECIPES 108

- *Roasted Asparagus w/ Lemon Vinaigrette* *108*
- *Garlic and Chickpea Soup* *110*
- *Colorful Veggie Detox Salad* *111*
- *Silky Cauliflower Soup* *112*
- **Cucumber Kimchi** *113*
- *Goat Cheese Asparagus Soufflés* *114*
- *Liver and Onions* *116*

MANAGE YOUR MICROBIOMES

- Pesto Tilapia 117
- Turkey Chili 118
- Roasted Garlic Cabbage 120
- Roasted Sage and Lemon Chicken 121
- Eggplant Chicken Stew 122
- Crock Pot Chili 124
- Shrimp Fried Cauliflower Rice 125
- Chicken w/ Peppers 126
- Warm Lemon Chicken 128
- **Coconut Chicken** 129
- Chicken Bruschetta 130
- Fried Salmon Fillets 131
- Zucchini Ribbon Salad 132
- MICROBIOME DIET SNACKS 133
  - Roasted Sweet Potato Chips 133
  - Roasted Asparagus 134
  - Guacamole w/ Vegetables 135
  - Kale Chips 136
  - Hard-Boiled Eggs w/ Avocado 137
  - Healthy Fried Plantain 138
  - Pickled Veggies 139
  - Stuffed Celery Bites 140
  - Pesto-Stuffed Mushrooms 141
  - Healthy Sautéed Kale 142
  - Vinegar & Salt Kale Chips 143
  - Squash Fries 144
  - Spinach Cake 145
  - Carrot French Fries 146
  - Roasted Balsamic Beets 147
  - Candied Macadamia Nuts 148
  - Fig Tapenade 149
  - Veggie Snack 150
  - Guacamole Deviled Eggs 151
  - Curried Roasted Cauliflower 152
  - Healthy Spiced Nuts 154
  - Sesame Crackers 155
- MICROBIOME DIET DRINKS 157
  - Fruity Kefir Smoothie 157
  - Healthy Gut Smoothie 158

MANAGE YOUR MICROBIOMES

The Best Gut Health Smoothie 159
Berry & Flax Smoothie 160
Happy Gut Energy Smoothie 161
Chia Pineapple Colada Kefir 162
Mango Green Tea 163
Tasty Stomach Healing Juice 164
Gut Cleansing Juice 165
Gut Healing Coconut Water Kefir Delight 166
Almond Butter Chocolate Smoothie 167
Delicious Strawberry Punch 168
Citrus Punch 169
Healthy Smoothie 170
Gingery Grape Juice 171
Detox Blend 172
Fat-Burner Detox Juice 173
Excellent Detoxifier 174
Garlicky Green Juice 175
Brighten-Up Juice 176
The Super-8 Detox Juice 177
Tropical Dream 178
Skin Soother Juice 179
Smooth Skin Juice 180
Berricious Smoothie 181
Cocoa Bliss 182
Lean Detox Smoothie 183
Super Detox Smoothie 184
Gingery Pineapple Paradise 185
Date Orange Smoothie 186
The Super Cleanser 187
Berry Magic Juice 188
Citrus Drink 189
Strawberry Papaya Smoothie 190
Wonder Cleanser 191
Papaya & Pear Detox Juice 192
Mint & Cucumber Detox Juice 193
Apple Cider Vinegar & Grape Juice 194

PARTING SHOT… **195**

MANAGE YOUR MICROBIOMES

PART ONE: INTRODUCTION

We've all heard of the phrase that *'money makes the world go round'*, but I like to think that it is actually food that makes the world go round. Food nourishes all the cells in your body allowing them to function optimally and providing you with the energy to perform all your daily activities.

However, our lives today have become so busy that we have forgotten the sanctity of food only to choose convenience. Given the option to make your food after a loooong workday or simply dial in dinner from your favorite restaurant, most of us would rather order in.

Before we know it, this seemingly harmless practice of ordering in food turns into a vicious unhealthy cycle and we have to pay a hefty price with our health. It's no secret that the escalating number of chronic illnesses that seem to be attacking the human race right, left and center is mostly attributed to unhealthy eating habits.

Diet and nutrition is one of the most dynamic topics that is constantly evolving. Nearly every day there is a new diet that hits the nutrition world promising to be the ultimate health booster and weight loss magic wand.

There is no denying that keeping up with the latest fitness and nutrition news can be an uphill task but in this book, we are going to look at nutrition basics that will help you sort through nutrition advice and research, what to keep and what to throw out.

We will take a stepwise approach in understanding why the microbiome diet is the best way for humans to feed, the role it plays in restoring health and offering sustainable weight loss. To top it all, we are also going to feature super healthy and super tasty microbiome recipes that will turn you into a super chef!

What Is The Microbiome Diet?

Did you know that microbiome is the key to healthy, fastest weight loss and impressive improvements in general health, energy, mental function and mood?

Before we go any further, let us first look into what microbiomes really are.

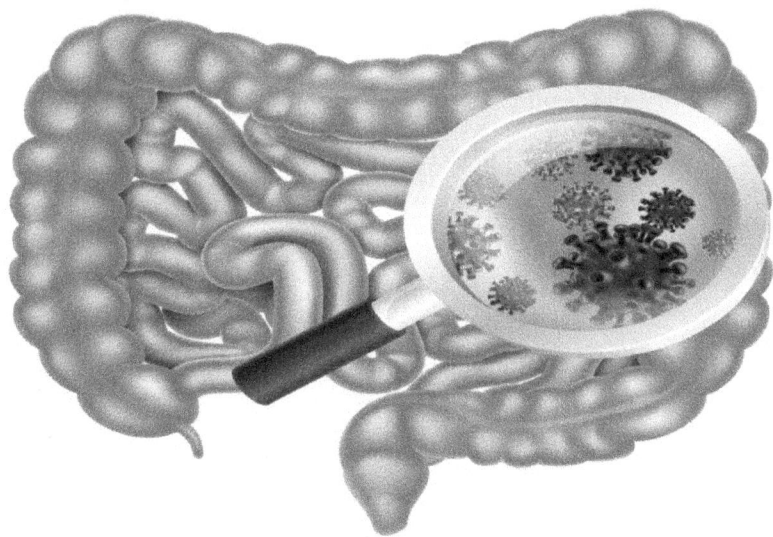

Definition:

These are trillions of tini-tiny microbes that live within your intestines to help you extract the vital nutrients from your food as well as exerting great influence over your hormones, metabolism, genes and also cravings.

The microbiome diet incorporates these biological breakthroughs into an effective program that guarantees fast, super healthy and permanent weight loss. Lots of fresh, wholesome fruits and veggies, whole grains and legumes are the perfect microbiome food.

MANAGE YOUR MICROBIOMES

We are going to delve deeper into the type of foods making up the microbiome diet and later we are going to enjoy sumptuous microbiome recipes that are not only tasty but that will also help you lose weight once and for all!

MANAGE YOUR MICROBIOMES

It all starts in your gut!

Hippocrates, a man considered to be the father of healthy nutrition, back in the day discovered the importance of the microbiome diet and went ahead to say, **"let thy food be thy medicine and thy medicine be thy food."** When you think about this statement and the effect it has on your body, you realize that every organ in your body relies on nutritious food for it to function optimally.

So, what actually happens when your digestive system is compromised and cannot absorb a good percentage of the nutrients you eat? Well, your organs are slowly going to be deprived and that's when you start complaining of not feeling too well and if you don't do anything about this, well, you'll basically end up with a full blown illness.

Way back in the day when our ancestors were hunters and gatherers, they ate nutrition rich foods that kept them in tip top shape. It is time for us now to reclaim our health by following suit. Don't get me wrong, I am not suggesting we start wearing animal skin or running around with spears looking for game meat, no, we have no shortage of food options; what we need to do is make health conscious food choices.

Has the microbiome diet been around all this time?

Yes!

Fresh fruit, vegetables and whole foods have been around for years and years but honestly speaking, we need them today more than ever before. Thousands of years ago, a Dutch seaman discovered the amazing health benefits of sauerkraut and always carried jars of sauerkraut during his sea voyages to prevent scurvy.

The Asian cultures, more specifically, the Chinese and Japanese have been eating fresh fruit and veggies as well as fermented veggies for centuries. Is it a coincidence that these two make the longest living societies in the whole world? I highly doubt it!

MANAGE YOUR MICROBIOMES

About 7 years ago, the World Health Organization followed the lifestyles of today's modern cultures in the bid to identify the healthiest and longest living cultures.

They found that the Japanese consumed large amounts of vegetables, fresh and fermented, ocean herbs, ginger and green tea. As a result, they have the healthiest and longer life spans, compared to other cultures in the world.

Sadly, America did not make it even to the top 20 is of the world's healthiest cultures. Fried and over-processed foods are no doubt the reason for this. The everyday American diet is fast, laden with unhealthy fats, genetically modified and over-processed. It's therefore no wonder that chronic illnesses such as diabetes, heart problems, obesity and many more are at an all-time high.

What happened to our diet?

The reason why more and more people are becoming increasingly sick is that the amount of enzymes and probiotics that promote healthy gut bacteria in our food has been slowly declining over the years. Take an example from yogurt, today we have pasteurized yogurt which has replaced the naturally fermented yogurt; traditional lacto-fermented veggies have been replaced by vinegar based fermented veggies…the list is endless.

Years back, grains were very safe to eat; they were soaked, sprouted and fermented for the highest microbiome potency making the grains 100% fit for consumption as the above processes neutralized the anti-nutrients found in gains. But, today, most of us buy canned beans without fully understanding the processes they have undergone and how fit for consumption they are.

It is time we embraced some of the good food habits that our ancestors used. The microbiome diet is focused on restoring your health to near perfection and in the process it helps you attain your healthy weight. My first piece of advice is go natural in all your food choices and as much as possible try to ensure your food sources are organic.

Superfoods to Help With Gut Bacteria

Is it true that healthy gut bacteria will help me lose weight and give me great health?

In a nutshell – YES!

So, what's the best way to build up on the bacteria that calls you home, aka, a robust microbiome?

These amazing superfoods!

- ❖ *Leeks*

Leeks are rich in flavonoids, dietary fiber, and manganese, which produce high quantities of vitamin A that does a great job of healing your gut wall and produces digestive enzymes to ease the digestion process.

❖ *Radishes*

These veggies are endowed with a compound known as arabiongalactans, which is an amazing food for the good bacteria in your intestinal tract.

❖ *Jerusalem Artichokes*

MANAGE YOUR MICROBIOMES

These artichokes are laden with inulin, a common fiber in fruits and vegetables. Inulin is a natural prebiotic that has zero calories but leaves you feeling satisfied. It constitutes about 19% of the total weight of Jerusalem artichokes.

❖ *Carrots*

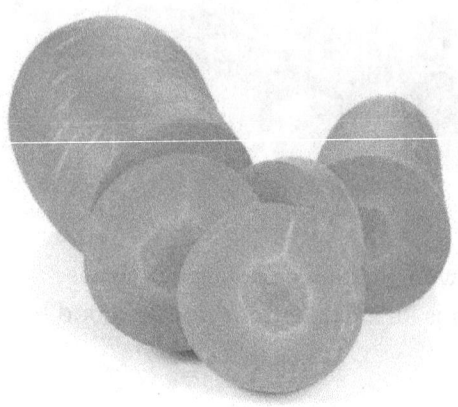

These root veggies are endowed with natural prebiotics similar to those in radishes. Additionally, carrots contain carotenoids and vitamins that help heal your gut wall and your skin as well.

❖ *Asparagus*

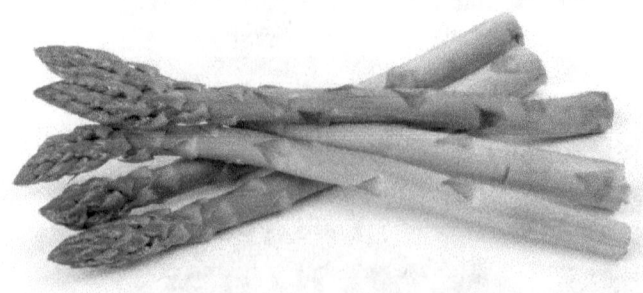

Asparagus contains multiple nutrients that aid in healing your gut wall, rich in inulin, leaves you feeling satisfied thanks to its high dietary fiber content, helps you lose weight and is great food for the microbiome and digestive enzymes.

❖ *Garlic*

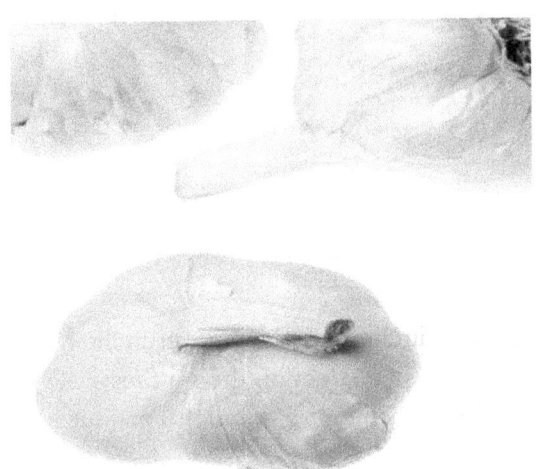

This is one of the most amazing prebiotics. It has an incredible effect on your immunity and it helps your microbiome to proliferate. Garlic additionally does an amazing job of fighting off unfriendly gut bacteria.

To be safe, you'd better start walking around with your toothpaste!

❖ *Jicama*

This root veggie is endowed with inulin, satisfies your crunchy food craving and more so has an impressive effect on the synthesis of important compounds that stimulate the microbiome to produce good bacteria.

❖ *Turmeric*

This spice is a natural anti-inflammatory that naturally heals your gut, promotes brain function and feeds your microbiome.

MANAGE YOUR MICROBIOMES

These are just a few of the superfoods that help gut bacteria flourish. We are going to look at other amazing foods in our recipe section later in the book.

Probiotic Foods

In the past few years, there has been a growing interest in the probiotic foods and supplements, thanks to studies indicating that beneficial bacteria help treat and prevent a wide range of ailments: from candidiasis to chronic inflammation –the root cause of cancer, heart disease and diabetes.

Regardless of the hype, it is true that probiotic foods have been around for the longest time. Studies show that fermented beverages were found in the ancient Babylon city about 5000 years ago.

Your gut is home to million bacteria, some bad and some good. Studies show that the more good bacteria your gut has, the stronger your immune will be.

Often referred to as "good bacteria", probiotics are beneficial gut bacteria that help your body to absorb essential vitamins and minerals, including vitamins A, D, E, and K, and iron, calcium, and chromium, just to mention a few.

The Health Benefits of Probiotics

The following are the health benefits associated with adding probiotics to your daily diet.

- Boost immune system
- Helps alleviate negative effects of taking different types of antibiotics
- Increase the ability to digest food
- Calm colon irritation after surgery
- Help reduce lactose intolerance
- Promotes healthy skin in young people
- Remedy for halitosis (bad breath)

- Alleviates many digestive disorders such as IBS, diarrhea, and constipation
- Promotes nutrient assimilation from food
- Reduces incidences of candidiasis, vaginitis and yeast infections
- Promotes calcium absorption
- Promotes vitamin B synthesis

Who Should Take Probiotics?

Candidiasis suffers need supplemental probiotics to replenish beneficial intestinal bacteria and rebuild their immune system. However, they are not the only ones who need probiotics –everyone who leads a high-stress lifestyle, eats processed food, or is exposed to a toxic environment would benefit from probiotics.

This is particularly true if you have frequent colds; you're taking strong antibiotics, or experience symptoms of candida. Probiotics perform nay important functions and without them, your body cannot function properly.

Top Probiotic Foods You Are Not Eating

If you're eating yogurt as the only probiotic food, then you are missing out on a whole lot of healthy fermented foods out there. Include these probiotics unto your diet to boost your gut –and overall –well-being.

Now let us look at some of the probiotic foods that have been eaten from around the world for centuries.

MANAGE YOUR MICROBIOMES

Kimchi

Another one of the best probiotic foods, kimchi is a popular Korean pickled dish that has received a wide acceptance by many cultures outside Asia. Kimchi is made by combining a main ingredient such as cabbage with a wide range if seasonings and ingredients, like garlic, carrot, radish, hot pepper flakes, onion, ginger, fish sauce and salt. The mixture is then fermented for days or even weeks.

Baechu is the most common type of kinchi –it is made with Chinese cabbages. However, many other kimchi variations are made with radishes, leeks, eggplants, cucumbers and other season vegetables.

The liberal use of red chili pepper makes kimchi a very spicy dish.

How to Eat:

Kimchi can be consumed in many ways –it can be used as a condiment. However, you need to know that due to its spiciness, whatever food you combine with kimchi will most likely end up with an overpowering taste –hot! I love this – you may not.

You should always add kimchi last in your cooking process and avoid overcooking to prevent loss of beneficial enzymes.

Health Benefits:

Kimchi is a rich source of lactobacillus kimchii, a bacterium that is very beneficial to your gastrointestinal and immune systems. The traditional kimchi made with Chinese cabbage, pepper, onion, ginger, garlic, and carrot is also rich in iron, calcium, beta-carotene, and vitamins A, C, B1, and B2.

Where to Buy:

If you have no time to make your own kimchi at home, go for kimchi that isn't too salty and spicy in an Asian market or your grocery store

Fact:

Although Korea is the origin of Kimchi, Japan is the largest exporter of Kimchi. Japan exports its own version of Kimchi.

MANAGE YOUR MICROBIOMES

Miso

Miso is an indispensable dark brown or white paste with a buttery texture made by fermenting brown rice, barley, soy bean or any other grain with a fungus called aspergillus oryzae (or koji in Japan). It's used in almost all Japanese kitchens as a seasoning. Usually, the darker the color of miso, the stronger and saltier the flavor.

How to Use:

Miso is very easy to make. Dissolve one or more tablespoon of miso in a pan of water filled with seaweed, tofu, and other ingredients to make soup.

Miso is not limited to making soups –it's used in Japan in many ways, including spreading on snacks made with pounded rice. You can also spread miso on toasts instead of butter or salt.

Just like many probiotic foods, miso should be added to dishes just before being removed from heat to preserve koji cultures and to retain nutrients.

Health Benefits:

Miso is a rich source of readily absorbable protein and vitamin B12. It is also rich in manganese, copper and zinc.

Where to Buy:

Miso can be found in almost all supermarkets. There are also organic varieties of miso for those who prefer greener and non-GMO products.

Fact:

Soy sauce or tamari is a byproduct left during the fermentation process of miso.

Tempeh

Originated from Indonesia, tempeh is a wonderful substitute for meat. It's a fermented, probiotic rich grain made from soy beans.

How to Eat:

It's a vegetarian food that can be eaten crumbled on salads, baked or sautéed. It can also be stir-fried with fresh vegetables as an alternative to meat. You can also use tempeh to make meatless burgers.

Health Benefits:

Tempeh is a good source of vitamin B12. It also contains *Rhizopus oligosporus*, a bacterium that produces a form of antibiotic that fights bacteria that cause sepsis and pneumonia.

Fact:

In addition to soybeans, there are less common varieties of tempeh that are made by mixing soy and grains, as well as other legumes.

Where to Buy:

Tempeh can be found in many supermarkets, often in the freezer compartments. You can also find it in Asian stores and healthy food stores.

Sauerkraut:

This is a western counterpart of Asian kimchi, except that it contains less seasonings and ingredients than kimchi. Popular among Europeans and Americans, sauerkraut typically contains shredded cabbage and salt as main ingredients. It's made by fermenting salted cabbage without adding vinegar or any starter for at least two weeks.

How to Eat:

Sauerkraut pairs perfectly with savory dishes and is usually served as a side dish in restaurants and even homes. It's a versatile dish that can be added to any food to give an acidic edge.

Health Benefits:

Just like its Asian counterpart, sauerkraut is a rich source of digestive enzymes and vitamin C. Sauerkraut juice is known to treat gastrointestinal conditions such as constipation and diarrhea.

Fact:

The first sauerkraut is said to originate from China, with some people saying that it was invented by Qin Shi Huangdi, the first emperor who unified China, while others saying it was invented by the founder of Mongol Empire –Genghis Khan.

Where to Buy:

Look for sauerkraut in your local supermarket or grocery store. However, nothing beats the homemade sauerkraut. You can check out online guides on how to make sauerkraut.

Kefir

Kefir is a well-known health beverage used in many European countries including Russia, Romania, Poland, Norway, Hungary, Finland, Ukraine and Sweden. It's made by fermenting the mixture of cow, sheep, or goat's milk and kefir grains. This probiotic-rich beverage is suitable for those who are lactose intolerant. Kefir is thicker than milk with a tart taste and a slight hint of alcohol. There are two types of kefir: milk kefir, which is the dairy version, and water kefir, non-dairy version.

How to Drink:

Milk kefir is often used like normal milk and thus, can be used as a substitute for milk in sauces, dressings, smoothies and other recipes.

Health Benefits:

Milk protein in kefir is more readily absorbed by the body than that contained in normal milk, thanks to the yeast and beneficial bacteria. Lactobacillus delbrueckii and lactobacillus kefiranofaciens, the bacteria in kefir grains, produce a gel-like polysaccharide known as kefiran. Kefiran exhibits anti-inflammatory and anti-tumor properties. It is also known to reduce bad cholesterol levels, blood glucose and blood pressure.

Fact:

The tribal people living in the Caucasus Mountains considered kefir grains a gift from God and the secret behind making kefir was guarded with one's life.

Where to Buy:

You can find recipes for making kefir all over the internet. Water and milk kefir grains can also be bought online.

MANAGE YOUR MICROBIOMES

Kombucha

Kombucha is a Chinese refreshing beverage made by fermenting sweetened black tea. Kombucha originated in China and dates back 2,000 years. The refreshing beverage is made by fermenting sweetened black tea.

How to Eat:

You can add kombucha to your salads instead of vinegar. It can also be used to marinate meats and fish. Try making frozen treats by blending kombucha with juices or fruits.

Health Benefits:

Kombucha has antibiotic properties, which makes it effective in fighting a range of pathogens. It also serves as a detoxifier to your body.

MANAGE YOUR MICROBIOMES

Where to Buy:

Get Kombucha in the refrigerated section of your grocery store.

Yogurt

Live-cultured yogurt is one of the best probiotic foods. It made by adding "good" bacteria to milk. The milk is then fermented to form a tangy flavored thick drink.

How to Eat:

You can drink yogurt as it is or add to smoothies, parfaits and other recipes.

Health Benefits:

Yogurt is a probiotic food with many health benefits behind it. It's high in protein, calcium, and vitamin B12. Yogurt boasts many health benefits including boosting immune system, preventing yeast infections, lowering serum cholesterol, and helping overcome lactose intolerance.

Where to Buy:

Yogurt is found in almost all supermarkets and healthy food stores. Always go for the yogurt brands made from goat's milk infused with more forms of probiotics such as acidophilus or lactobacillus.

Fun Facts:

Yogurt was first made by accident – many historical records attribute the origin of yogurt to the primitive methods of storing milk in containers that were made from animal stomachs. The enzymes from the animal stomachs would curdle milk, leading to what we know as yogurt.

Natto

This is a Japanese food made from fermented soybeans. Natto contains *bacillus subtilis*, a bacterial strain that gives natto its characteristic stringy consistency. This probiotic-rich food has a unique pungent smell and an equally distinctive flavor not found in other probiotic foods.

How to Eat:
Traditionally, Japanese consume Natto with rice for breakfast. It's mixed with rice and some soy sauce. Today, natto can also be found in many other products such as natto salad, natto burrito and natto sushi. Yum yum!

Health Benefits:
Just like other soybean products, natto is a rich source of protein. Research suggests that natto is also high in vitamin K which is important for blood clotting and protection against osteoporosis

and bone fractures. It is also rich in nattokinase, an enzyme that dissolves blood clots in animal tests.

Where to Buy:
Find natto in the freezer compartments in Asian grocery stores. You can also find digestive types of natto in many major supermarkets.

Fact:
The former child prodigy, Michael Kearney who was recorded in the Guinness Book as the youngest person graduating from the University of South Alabama (graduated at the age of 10 and taught college students at the age of 17), was said to be fed with natto while young by his Japanese mother.

MANAGE YOUR MICROBIOMES

Prebiotic Foods

Prebiotics are partially digestible or non-digestible food ingredients that serve as food for the beneficial gut bacteria (probiotics). Along with probiotics, prebiotics are functional foods that provide health benefits that go beyond the basic nutrition. While they are widely available as supplements, prebiotics also occur naturally in several common foods containing high fiber content.

Meet the Prebiotics

Making up prebiotic family are a number of fibrous elements occurring naturally in foods you consume. The common prebiotics are the closely related fructo-oligosaccharides and inulins, both of which usually pass through the GI without being digested or absorbed into the body, making them great prebiotics. These prebiotics pass through the intestines to the colon where they stimulate the growth of probiotics occurring naturally in the human GI –bifidobacteria and other beneficial microorganisms.

Symbiosis of Probiotics and Prebiotics

Studies have shown strong evidence of a symbiotic relationship between probiotics and prebiotics. A recent study has shown that the combination of probiotics Bifidobacterium lactis and lactobacillus and prebiotics oligofructose and inulin significantly reduces colon tumors in test animals. These studies suggest that probiotics and prebiotics work hand in hand to promote overall well-being. Health experts recommends including adequate amounts of prebiotics in your daily diet to promote the health of probiotic flora occurring naturally in your GI tract.

MANAGE YOUR MICROBIOMES

Foods Rich in Prebiotics

Foods rich in prebiotics include chicory, asparagus, Jerusalem artichoke, dandelion root, leeks, garlic and onions.

Other Health Benefits

While they are best known to promote the growth of probiotics or the beneficial bacteria in your GI tract, prebiotics have other health benefits that make them a great addition to a healthy diet.

Of great importance among these health benefits is the increased calcium absorption. Prebiotics are also known to prevent inflammatory bowel disease as well as colon cancer.

Top Prebiotic Foods

Food	Prebiotic Fiber by Weight(% per 100 grams)	Mount required to achieve daily serving of prebiotic fiber
Raw Jerusalem artichoke	31.5%	¾ oz. (19g)
Raw chicory root	64.6%	1/3 oz.(9.3g)
Raw garlic	17.5%	1.2 oz. (34.3g)
Raw dandelion greens	24.3%	Just under 1 oz. (24.7g)
Raw asparagus	5%	¼ pound (120g)
Raw onion	8.6%	2.5 oz. (69.8g)
Raw leek	11.7%	1.8 oz. (51.3g)
Raw wheat bran	5%	¼ pound (120g)
Raw banana	1%	1.3 pounds (600g)

MANAGE YOUR MICROBIOMES

The Plant Based Diet and Micro Diversity

When you hear the term plant based diet, the first thing that automatically comes to mind is going completely vegan and then decide, that's not happening! While going completely vegetarian or vegan can be very healthy and perfectly nutritious, eating a plant based diet doesn't necessarily mean swearing off eggs and meat forever. It simply means trying to fill up your plate with real, wholesome plant based sources.

The focal point of a plant based diet is nutrient dense, natural and wholesome foods such as fruits, beans, lentils, peas, seeds, soy beans, nuts, veggies and wholegrains. At the same time, this diet minimizes on processed foods and oils as well as animal products.

A plant based diet offers a great and well balanced macro and micro diversity, that is, carbohydrates, protein, fat, vitamins and minerals.

Plant based nutrition is also a very good source of phytochemicals – naturally occurring compounds present in plant based foods that protect your body from chronic illnesses such as diabetes, cancer, heart diseases and so on.

When shopping for a plant based diet, your grocery cart should be filled with plenty of colorful fruits and veggies that are mostly non-starchy, whole grain products. The key is to get food that is in its natural state or closest to its naturally occurring state.

It has been shown that a plant based diet is what microbiomes thrive on best due its micro diversity. Radiant, young skin, permanent weight loss, great health… are some of the benefits you stand to gain from switching to a plant based diet.

Different bacteria feed on different foods ad by increasing the variety of plant based foods you also increase the micro diversity of your microbiome and thus stand to gain more health wise.

Microbiome Diet and Weight Loss

Looking down the street as you go about your errands you will notice that the number of obese and overweight people is at an alarming high today compared to any other point in time. What's most worrying is that our kids too haven't been spared and it is now common to see an eight year old complaining of joint pains because they carry too much weight than can be supported by their tiny bones.

It's a no brainer that the western diet has greatly fueled the rise in obesity. We are at point where we can no longer look the other side and brush off this issue. Our kids are getting into puberty way before their time and it's hard not to worry that if our kids are growing so fast, does it mean they are also going to die when they are at their prime?

This is not a question that anyone would like to answer and it's high time we reversed all this using the microbiome diet. We start by answering this question;

Does Bad Bacteria Make You Fat?

Let us answer this question with another question; what drives tooth decay? A typical western diet is overloaded with sugar, sodium and fat with the worst part being that most of these foods are over processed and so you end up stacking on truckloads of calories with zero nutritional value.

These over-processed foods are the food of choice for nasty microbes that start by causing tooth decay and continue with the damage right down into your digestive tract. Once in your gut, these microbes release endotoxins, which are toxic byproducts that corrode your gut walls giving you a leaky gut syndrome.

MANAGE YOUR MICROBIOMES

With time, these endotoxins make their way into your blood stream now that your gut walls have become porous. Your body being super smart launches a protective mechanism by triggering inflammation, which affects the functioning of your brain.

When inflammation occurs, the hypothalamus – located in the central part of your brain and what controls your appetite, rewires your metabolic system so it redirects most of the energy produced to fight off whatever is attacking your body and causing the inflammation.

The result is an increased appetite, a spike in insulin production and storage of extra fat. These three are the driving factors for diabetes, obesity, heart disease and a myriad of other chronic illnesses.

Back to our question, a lack of friendly bacteria that promote healthy gut flora inevitably leads to an uncontrollable weight gain.

It's not all downhill from here. The good news is that using the microbiome diet, this vicious cycle can be reversed. What you will need to do is cut out processed and refined products from your diet. Introduce natural and organic food products. If you can't do without pasta, make your own using whole grain flour. By doing this, you are going to gradually repopulate your gut with friendly bacteria and also create an acidic environment in your gut that will kill the bad bacteria.

Your stomach is like a rainforest, the home to thriving ecosystem of friendly bacteria and sometimes harmful bacteria. Recent scientific research has shown that about 95% of microbiome in your body is found in your gut. It thus makes a lot of sense that it regulates your weight.

The more diverse the friendly bacteria in your gut, the less likely you are to be overweight or obese. Fresh and natural plant based food is the primary food for the microbiome. These healthy bugs primarily feed on the sugar and starch in your food and so reducing your chances of adding weight.

Make your diet interesting by constantly changing it up to allow diverse healthy bacteria to thrive and weight issues will no longer be part of the list of your problems!

You are probably wondering why we call the good bacteria friendly. Well, the reason is, good bacteria feeds on the sugar and starches in your food thus creating probiotics, beneficial enzymes and omega 3 fatty acids that aid digestion, protect you from diseases and help you lose weight.

Gut Bacteria and Food Cravings

Are you having a hard time avoiding the emergency dietary siren call of chocolate chip cookies or pretzels? Blame the bacteria in your gut!

Did you know that your gut acts like a mini brain? Well, it produces a wide variety of hormones and it also has many of the same neurotransmitters as your brain. The walls of your gut contain neurons in in a distributed network and this is how it communicates to your brain. The bacteria in your gut can sway how full you feel, can tell your brain the foods to crave and they can even change your taste receptors, making some foods seem more tasty and more appealing than others

The microbiome in your gut has been shown to determine the types of food you crave. Just as you might have thought, bad bacteria make you crave bad food and good bacteria make you crave good food. The microbiome can therefore manipulate you into eating or not eating certain types of food.

For example, if your gut is filled with sugar dependent bacteria, these microbes would be under strong pressure to manipulate you to eat more of sugar-filled foods and thus the cravings.

MANAGE YOUR MICROBIOMES

Now, the good news is that you can change your microbiome makeup in just 24 hours by swapping your diet in favor of a more natural plant based diet thus replacing the microbes craving crappy food. The less junk you eat the less cravings you are going to have for junk food. So the next time you crave junk food, get healthy bacteria!

Microbiome Diet For Certain Conditions

'*Let thy food be thy medicine and thy medicine be thy* food', these are the wise words by the Father of healthy nutrition, Hippocrates. The truth is, all maladies start in the gut. When you think about it, each organ in your body, big or small, relies on food for it to function optimally.

So, what do you think will happen when your digestive system gets impaired and can no longer absorb most of the nutrients you eat? It's pretty obvious that your organs and cells are going to be deprived of very essential nutrients and minerals and before long; you are going to start feeling unwell.

A Healthy Gut + Good Quality Food = Great Health

Think of your body as a tree and your digestive system as its root network. For your tree to grow healthy and strong, it needs great nourishment, water, lots and lots of sunshine and air. Likewise, your body needs first grade nutrition for it to flourish. If your digestive system is overloaded with over-processed foods, no doubt your organs are going to start complaining and if you don't nip the bud in time you are going to have to deal with overstrained organs in the form of chronic illnesses.

Your gut is in constant battle with harmful bacteria, fungi, viruses, protozoa and worms to keep you healthy and disease free. It does this by using stomach acid and friendly bacteria. Your diet should be aimed at helping your gut and what better way than following the microbiome diet?

Before we go any further, it is important to note that if your gut does not have the capacity to fight off disease causing pathogens,

MANAGE YOUR MICROBIOMES

they can literally take over the whole of your digestive system, corrode your intestinal walls and eventually leave your tract inflamed and with autoimmune diseases that are such a pain to treat.

The microbiome diet is the holy grail of healthy gut flora and your overall gut health. For a long time, medical professionals viewed microbes as terrible things that should be gotten rid of. After all, viruses give us the flu and measles; bacteria give us food poisoning and strep throat.

But, with increased research, it has been found that most microbes actually don't make us sick and a good percentage are vital for our health. It is now evident that subtle imbalances in our microbiome causes disease and how by restoring balance may lead to cure and even prevention of disease.

Here are a few of the health conditions that involve your microbiome:

- Asthma and allergies
- Acne
- Autism
- Antibiotic related diarrhea
- Autoimmune diseases and inflammation
- Anxiety
- Cancer
- Diabetes
- Dental cavities
- Depression
- Eczema
- Hardening of the arteries
- Gastric ulcer
- Malnutrition
- Inflammatory bowel illnesses

- Obesity

If you suffer from any of the above mentioned health conditions, visit your doctor in the presence of a nutritionist and deliberate on how you can incorporate the microbiome diet into your treatment plan to reduce symptoms and eventually eliminate the condition completely.

MANAGE YOUR MICROBIOMES

The Science behind the Microbiome Diet

Numerous scientific studies have shown that the bacteria community together with fungi, gut infections, parasites and viruses that occupy the ecosystem of your gut microbiome affects chronic illness, inflammation, arthritis, skin problems such as acne, eczema, psoriasis, autism, obesity, insulin resistance, autoimmunity, cancer, eating disorders, mood, dementia, depression and so much more.

This now makes so much sense because about 85% of our immune cells reside in the microbiome. Many of the mentioned diseases are unrelated but are caused by gut microbiome conflict – dysbiosis, which in actual fact is the imbalance of the microbiome.

The bottom line is if you want to solve your emotional, health and mental issues, your starting point should be your gut. In light of this, a diet that is protective of the gut microbiome should be your main focus.

- Eat lots of plant based foods with about 5-30 different varieties every week. The more the better.
- Sun and outdoor exposure also diversifies the microbiome.
- 7-9 hours of sleep yields a more diverse microbiome.
- Frequent exercise, preferably done outdoors will yield a diverse microbiome
- One alcoholic drink can be helpful to the gut microbiome but more than one may potentially reduce the diversity.
- Antibiotic drugs wipe out the microbiome with some people recovering relatively fast and others taking up to one year to fully recover.

We cannot assume the fact that the microbiome may just be the missing piece of the puzzle that will make personalized medicine effective!

MANAGE YOUR MICROBIOMES

Your evolving microbiome

Before birth when you are still in your mother's womb, you are practically sterile, that is, you have no microbes. But during the birthing process, microbes start colonizing your body. And, depending on how you were born, you are colonized by different types of microbes.

Your first dose of microbes comes from your mom:

Vaginal delivery – babies are covered in a film of microbes as they make their way through the birth canal. In the microbe mix are bacteria that will aid the baby in digesting his/her first meal.

Caesarean section delivery - babies are mostly colonized by skin microbes, which is a different set from those encountered in vaginal delivery.

After birth, babies continue picking up microbes not only from their moms but anyone else or thing that they come into contact with. These subtle differences between delivery types are measurable months later and may have long lasting impacts on health.

From there, what a child eats will continue affecting the microbiome. Breast fed babies have a more diverse microbiome compared to their formula fed counterparts. The first foods they are fed with also influence the microbiome with plant-based foods having a more positive effect on the microbiome.

In addition to feeding yourself well, you also have to consider your child and what's best for him/her. This way, you are potentially going to help protect your young ones from illnesses.

Making the Transition to the Microbiome Diet Easier

So far, we have established that you are what you eat and the bacteria in your gut microbiome too 'are what you eat'. The good thing is that gut microbiome is very responsive to diet change.

MANAGE YOUR MICROBIOMES

Within days of embracing a healthy plant based diet, a great variation in the abundance of these little friends is manifested.

Scientific studies show that this fast response by the gut microbiome to diet changes was essential to survival of the human race from the hunter and gatherer age. For our ancient ancestors, diet could be altered very fast and with very little transition.

Weeks of veggies, seeds, nuts and roots could be broken up by a sudden abundance of meat from a successful game hunt. The ability to rapidly change the gut microbiome was necessary to ensure optimal nutrient absorption from even the most unfamiliar and unusual foods. I guess we owe our ancestors one!

One thing to keep in mind is that although the microbiome was constantly changing, ALL foods were healthy. Today our diet is marred with truckloads of junk and though you may be in love with your chips, your gut microbiome is definitely not.

The good news is that all you need is to rid your kitchen of processed foods and restock it with healthy, nutrient dense, natural and wholesome foods. Well, easier said than done, right?

Waking up and deciding no chocolate, cookies, chips, cheese fries…from today is setting up you for failure. You should never make yourself feel deprived as this will only intensify cravings which almost inevitably followed by mad binge eating sprees.

So, what's the best way to transition into the microbiome diet?

Mindful eating is the answer. But, what does this mean?

The first thing you should do is recognize that your body is a temple that deserves the best and t be take good care of. Many of us are guilty of treating our bodies like a wood shed by stuffing it with tubs of ice cream, gallons of soda, buckets of fried chicken, boxes of cookies and chocolate and so much more. This not how to love yourself!

MANAGE YOUR MICROBIOMES

Treating your body like a temple means that you want to fill it with nutritious food to ensure it looks and feels great and operates optimally and this is the aim of mindful eating. Eating clean nutrient dense foods without feeling like you are punishing yourself.

Yes, sometimes you may feel like eating some ice cream or snack of choice. Instead of depriving yourself, go for the kid size option. This way, you will satisfy your craving without going overboard after that, try to compensate by exercising and eating clean afterwards.

Take it a day at a time, set yourself a goal that you can attain for one week. For example, I will reduce my meat eating days from 6 days in a week to three. The next week set another goal such as not taking cream in your coffee or replacing your coffee with green tea…slowly by slowly the microbiome in your gut will take notice and more friendly bacteria will populate your gut and actually change your cravings from junk food to super tasty plant based foods. From craving ice cream to a yummy fruit smoothie.

Don't believe me? You just have to try it out yourself with the tastiest microbiome recipes in our next section.

Fact:

Did you know that the average healthy adult carries about 2 kilograms of bacteria in the stomach? A good proportion of these bacteria are friendly and good for your gut health, so much so that were our guts a hundred percent sterile, we would die!

A very important point to note with regard to the microbiome diet is that it does not employ a 'one size fits all' technique. You could be a full vegan; a vegetarian who eats lots or fruits, legumes, nuts and grains; or you could be on a plant-based diet with moderate amounts of fish, chicken, lamb or beef and still be perfectly healthy.

MANAGE YOUR MICROBIOMES

The secret is to keep supporting your little buddies inside – your microbiome!

Let us now commence to the fun part, FOOD! Get your apron ready and let's get cooking!

MANAGE YOUR MICROBIOMES

PART TWO: THE MICROBIOME DIET RECIPES

Microbiome Breakfast Recipes

Vegetable Breakfast Bakes
This delicious veggie breakfast dish is made with fresh mushrooms, spinach, tomatoes and a microbiome super food, garlic.

Yield: 4 Servings

Total Time: 45 Minutes

Prep Time: 15 Minutes

Cook Time: 30 Minutes

Ingredients

- 4 large field mushrooms
- 8 tomatoes, halved
- 1 garlic clove, thinly sliced
- 2 tsp. extra virgin olive oil
- 200g bag spinach
- 4 eggs

Directions

Preheat your oven to 400°F.

Place tomatoes and mushrooms into four ovenproof dishes and divide garlic among the dishes; drizzle with extra virgin olive oil, salt and pepper. Bake for about 10 minutes.

In the meantime, place spinach in a colander and pour over boiling water until wilted. Squeeze out water and divide the spinach among the dishes.

MANAGE YOUR MICROBIOMES

Make a hole in the center of each dish and crack an egg into each hole. Continue baking for about 10 minutes more or until the egg is set.

Dill-Tomato Frittata

Tomatoes and dill lend an amazing flavor to the eggs in this recipe. The dish heats up nicely in the microwave.

Yields: 4 Servings

Total Time: 45 Minutes

Prep Time: 15 Minutes

Cook Time: 30 Minutes

Ingredients

- 8 free range eggs, beaten
- Coconut oil to grease pan
- 4 tomatoes, diced
- 1 tsp. red pepper flakes
- 2 garlic cloves, minced
- 2 tbsp. chopped fresh chives
- 2 tbsp. chopped fresh dill
- Salt and pepper

Directions

Preheat your oven to 325°F.

Spray a cast iron skillet or saucepan with olive oil spray.

In a bowl, whisk together eggs and the remaining ingredients until well blended.

Pour the mixture into the pan and bake for about 30 minutes or until cooked through. To serve, garnish with extra chives and dill.

MANAGE YOUR MICROBIOMES

Healthy Pumpkin Granola

This is an excellent recipe for homemade granola. Cranberries, dates, and almonds make this breakfast dish crunchy and irresistible! It is simple, fast, gluten free and vegan!

Yields: 4 Servings

Total Time: 1 Hour 15 Minutes

Prep Time: 15 Minutes

Cook Time: 1 Hour

Ingredients

- ½ cup coconut oil
- 1½ cup sliced almonds
- 1 cup almond meal
- ½ cup chopped dates
- 1 cup dried cranberries
- 1 cup pecans, chopped
- 1 cup pumpkin seeds
- 1½ cup chopped coconut flakes
- 1 tsp. cinnamon
- 1 tsp. pumpkin pie spice
- ½ cup pumpkin puree

Directions

Preheat your oven to 275°F. Line baking sheet with parchment paper.

Combine together dates, almond flour, coconut flakes, pumpkin seeds, cranberries, pecans and almonds in a bowl.

Stir in the wet ingredients until well combined.

MANAGE YOUR MICROBIOMES

Spread the mixture on the baking sheet and bake for about 1 hour, stirring after every 15 minutes.

Healthy Breakfast Porridge

This recipe presents the easiest way to start your day right. It's a colorful breakfast meal that you'll never get sick of eating.

Yields: 2 Servings

Total Time: 20 Minutes

Prep Time: 10 Minutes

Cook Time: 10 Minutes

Ingredients

- ½ cup almond milk
- 1 tsp. cinnamon
- ½ cup pecans
- ½ cup almonds
- ½ cup berries, plus extra to serve

Directions

Combine ingredients in a food processor and pulse until blended.

Heat the mixture in a saucepan until well cooked. Serve topped with more berries.

Smoked Salmon and Red Pepper Scramble

If you love scrambles, you'll never get enough of this dish. It's irresistibly delicious and healthy too!

Yields: 1 Serving

Total Time: 40 Minutes

Prep Time: 15 Minutes

Cook Time: 25 Minutes

Ingredients

- 1 tbsp. extra virgin olive oil
- 2 pieces smoked salmon, torn apart
- 2 organic eggs and 1 egg yolk, beaten
- ⅛ tsp. garlic powder
- ⅛ tsp. red pepper flakes
- 1 tbsp. chopped fresh dill
- Salt and pepper

Directions

Beat the eggs in a bowl; stir in garlic, dill, salmon, red pepper flakes, black pepper and salt until well combined.

Set a saucepan over low heat; add extra virgin olive oil. Once warm, add the egg mixture and cook, stirring until cooked through. Serve topped with roasted veggies.

Broccoli and Sausage Quiche

This is a versatile dish that goes from breakfast buffet to lunch or dinner table in a snap and is perfect when served with leafy green salad. The crust is paleo and very healthy.

Yields: 8 Slices

Total Time: 45 Minutes

Prep Time: 10 Minutes

Cook Time: 35 Minutes

Ingredients

- 9 free range eggs
- 2 tbsp. coconut oil
- 2 cups almond flour
- 1 cup broccoli
- ½ pound breakfast sausage
- 2 tbsp. water
- 1 tsp. sea salt

Directions

Cook the sausage and set aside.

Steam the broccoli and set aside.

Blend almond flour and sea salt in a food processor until well combined.

Add one egg and coconut oil and continue processing to form a ball.

Spread the dough on a quiche dish and top with broccoli and sausage.

MANAGE YOUR MICROBIOMES

In a bowl, whisk the remaining eggs with water and pour over the broccoli and sausage.

Bake at 350°F for about 35 minutes or until firm and cooked through.

Berry Omelet

A berry omelet recipe may not sound good to many because of its unusual blend of ingredients, but it is one of the gut-friendly recipes you just have to try.

Yields: 1 Serving

Total Time: 30 Minutes

Prep Time: 15 Minutes

Cook Time: 15 Minutes

Ingredients

- 175g chopped raspberries, blueberries and strawberries
- 1 large free range egg
- 1 tbsp. almond milk
- 100g sheep's milk cheese
- ½ tsp. rapeseed oil
- ¼ tsp. cinnamon

Directions

In a bowl, beat together the egg, milk and cinnamon until well blended.

Add oil to a nonstick pan set over medium heat. Add the egg mixture and swirl to cover the base evenly. Cook the egg mixture until set.

Transfer the omelet to a plate and sprinkle with cheese. Top with berries and roll up to serve.

Bacon & Pepper Frittata

Yields: 4 Servings

Total Time: 40 Minutes

Prep Time: 10 Minutes

Cook Time: 30 Minutes

Ingredients

- 6 strips bacon, cooked, crumbled
- 8 free-range eggs
- 1 tbsp. coconut oil
- 2 tbsp. green onion, chopped
- 1/2 yellow bell pepper, diced
- 1/2 green bell pepper, diced
- 1/2 red bell pepper, diced
- Sea salt
- Black pepper

Directions

Preheat your oven to 350°F.

Add coconut oil to a skillet set over medium heat.

Stir in peppers and sauté for 7 minutes or until translucent.

In the meantime, beat the eggs in a bowl and season with salt and pepper.

Add bacon to the skillet with peppers and cook for 2 minutes more. Stir in the eggs and cook for about 2 minutes or until set.

Transfer the skillet to the oven and bake for about 14 minutes.

Serve the frittata warm garnished with chopped green onions.

Basil Tomato Scramble

What a lighter twist on a tasty breakfast scramble for the vegetarians and calorie-conscious eaters! It's completely off the wall and tastes so great!

Yields: 2 Servings

Total Time: 20 Minutes

Prep Time: 10 Minutes

Cook Time: 10 Minutes

Ingredients

- 1 tbsp. coconut oil
- 1 tomato, diced
- 4 free-range eggs
- Sea salt
- Black pepper
- 3 basil leaves, minced

Directions

Add coconut oil to a skillet set over medium heat.

Beat the eggs in a bowl until frothy; stir in basil and tomato until well combined.

Gently add the egg mixture to the skillet with oil and cook to your desired doneness.

Transfer to serving plates and season with salt and pepper to serve.

MANAGE YOUR MICROBIOMES

Gut-Friendly Frittata

When it comes to an impromptu breakfast, nothing beats a frittata, an Italian version of a healthy omelet. This recipe relies on the convenience of spinach, which is not only delicious but also a great source of fiber.

Yields: 2 Servings

Total Time: 40 Minutes

Prep Time: 15 Minutes

Cook Time: 25 Minutes

Ingredients

- 1 pound spinach, sliced
- 6 organic eggs
- 1 small zucchini, sliced
- 2 tbsp. extra virgin olive oil
- 1 cup sliced onions
- ¼ cup grated sheep's milk cheese, divided
- 1 tsp. snipped tarragon
- 2 tbsp. cold water
- ½ tsp. sea salt
- ½ tsp. pepper

Directions

Preheat your oven to 475°F.

In a small bowl, beat together t eggs and cold water until well combined. Stir in 2 tablespoons cheese, tarragon and ½ teaspoon each of salt and black pepper. Set aside.

Add oil to a nonstick skillet set over medium heat; sauté onion for about 5 minutes or until translucent. Stir in zucchini and sauté for about 7 minutes or until lightly browned. Stir in spinach and cook for about 7 minutes or until wilted.

Evenly spread the veggies in the skillet and season with the remaining salt and pepper. Add the egg mixture and cook until the eggs start to set.

Sprinkle with the remaining cheese and bake in the preheated oven for about 5 minutes or until firm.

MANAGE YOUR MICROBIOMES

Berry & Cinnamon Smoothie

A fiber-rich and microbiome friendly beverage to go –perfect for breakfast!

Yields: 1 to 2 Servings

Total Time: 5 Minutes

Prep Time: 5 Minutes

Cook Time: 0 Minutes

Ingredients

- 1 cup frozen berries
- 1 cup kale
- ½ avocado
- 1 ½ cups coconut milk
- 5 drops vanilla extract
- ¼ tsp. cinnamon

Directions

Blend everything together until very smooth. Serve immediately.

Buttermilk Kefir Herb Biscuits

Just like the chocolate and peanut butter balls, these healthy gut-friendly biscuits are perfect for parties and sleepovers.

Total Time: 45 Minutes

Prep Time: 15 Minutes

Cook Time: 30 Minutes

Yields: 12 Servings

Ingredients

- ¾ cup of kefir
- 4 eggs
- ¾ cup coconut flour
- ¾ cup coconut oil
- ¾ cup tapioca flour
- 2 tbsp. raw honey
- 1 tsp. baking powder
- 1 tsp. kosher salt
- 1 tsp. parsley
- ½ tsp. baking soda
- 1 tsp. chopped fresh sage
- 1 tsp. fresh thyme

Directions

Preheat your oven to 350°F. Prepare a muffin tin by lining it with cupcake liners.

In a bowl, stir together tapioca flour, coconut flour, baking powder, salt and baking soda. With an electric mixer on high speed, whip together honey and butter until well blended.

MANAGE YOUR MICROBIOMES

Beat in eggs one at a time until well combined. Whip in a third of dry flour mixture until well blended. Whip in a third of kefir.

Repeat with the remaining flour mixture and kefir and whip in herbs.

Scoop the batter into cupcake liners and bake for about 28 minutes.

Sausage Spinach and Cheese Strata

This recipe is perfect for those who love meat at breakfast. It's made with microbiome super food, kefir. Fabulous!

Yields: 6 Servings

Total Time: 1 Hour 20 Minutes

Prep Time: 35 Minutes

Cook Time: 45 Minutes

Ingredients

- 14-16 ounces unflavored plain kefir
- 8 ounces sliced mushrooms
- 8 ounces breakfast sausage, sliced
- 6 large free range eggs
- ¼ tsp. onion powder
- ¼ tsp. garlic powder
- 12 ounces sheep's milk cheese, grated
- 3 to 5 ounces spinach, roughly chopped
- Black pepper
- Kosher salt
- ¼ tsp. thyme
- ¼ tsp. nutmeg
- 16 ounce loaf of gluten-free bread, cubed

Directions

Preheat your oven to 325°F.

Lightly coat a 9×10-inch spring form pan with olive oil cooking spray and line with parchment paper.

MANAGE YOUR MICROBIOMES

In a skillet, sauté mushrooms and sausage for a few minutes or until caramelized. Stir in onion, garlic, thyme and nutmeg powders; remove the pan from heat.

Arrange half of the bread cubes in a single layer in the prepared pan and top with third each of cheese and spinach; press down and spread evenly with mushroom mixture. Add another layer of spinach and cheese and press firmly. Add another layer of bread cubes and top with more cheese and spinach.

In a bowl, beat together eggs and kefir; pour over the strata and let stand to soak for about 5 minutes. Sprinkle with the remaining cheese and let stand for 15 more minutes.

Place the strata in the baking sheet and bake in the preheated oven for about 45 minutes. Serve warm.

Cultured Dairy Buckwheat Pancakes

These culture dairy buckwheat pancakes are great for breakfast or brunch. Serve them topped with caramelized onions for satisfying breakfast meal

Yields: 4 Servings

Total Time: 1 Hour 5 Minutes

Prep Time: 25Minutes

Cook Time: 40 Minutes

Ingredients:

- 1¼ cups milk kefir
- 1½ cups buckwheat flour
- 2 eggs, beaten
- ½ tsp. sea salt
- ½ tsp. baking soda
- ½ tsp. baking powder
- coconut oil
- ½ tsp. vanilla extract

Directions

In a bowl, mix together kefir and buckwheat flour until well combined. Let sit, covered, for about 12 hours.

When ready, preheat the pan over medium low heat.

In the meantime, combine buckwheat flour mixture with the remaining ingredients until well blended.

Add coconut oil to the pan and

MANAGE YOUR MICROBIOMES

Ladle three tablespoons of batter into the oil for each pancake. Cook until the top dries out, for about 5 minutes. Flip over and continue cooking for 2 more minutes or until well browned.

Salmon Egg Sandwich

If you want to wake up to a breakfast meal that is not only protein-packed but also palate-pleasing, make this salmon egg sandwich.

Yields: 1 sandwich

Total Time: 15 minutes

Prep Time: 10 Minutes

Cook Time: 5 Minutes

Ingredients

- 1 ounce smoked salmon
- 1/2 tsp. capers, rinsed and chopped
- 2 large egg whites, beaten
- 1 tbsp. chopped red onion
- 1/2 tsp. extra-virgin olive oil
- Sea salt
- 1 slice tomato
- 1 gluten-free muffin, split and toasted

Directions

Add oil to a skillet set over medium heat. Stir in onion and sauté for about 1 minute or until tender. Stir in egg whites, capers and salt and cook for about 30 seconds or until egg whites are set.

Make the sandwich by layering the egg whites, tomato and smoked salmon on the muffin.

MANAGE YOUR MICROBIOMES

Asparagus with Poached Egg

A sweet start to a healthy breakfast, this amazing breakfast meal tastes good any way you choose to serve it –at room temperature or warm.

Yields: 4 Servings

Total Time: 25 Minutes

Prep Time: 5 Minutes

Cook Time: 20 Minutes

Ingredients

- 2 pounds asparagus, trimmed
- 1/3 cup finely grated sheep's milk cheese
- 4 organic free range eggs
- 2 tsp. apple cider vinegar

Directions

Bring a pan of salted water to a rolling boil; add asparagus and cook until tender crisp and bright green, for about 3 minutes. Transfer the cooked asparagus to a plate and keep warm.

Add apple cider vinegar to the pan with salted water and lower heat to medium lo.

Crack an egg into a bowl; stir the boiling water with a spoon to make a whirlpool. Pour the egg in the middle of the whirlpool and cook for about 4 minutes or until cooked through.

Transfer the cooked egg to a plate and keep warm. Repeat the procedure with the remaining eggs.

Divide the cooked asparagus among the serving plate and top each with one egg. Sprinkle with salt, pepper and cheese to serve.

Spinach, Leek, & Feta omelets

Shake up your morning meal routine with this healthy omelet. It will definitely become a family favorite!

Yields: 4 Servings

Total Time: 25 Minutes

Prep Time: 15 Minutes

Cook Time: 10 Minutes

Ingredients

- 2 leeks, thinly sliced
- 3 tbsp. extra virgin olive oil, plus more for drizzling
- 6 organic free range eggs
- 1/4 cup sheep's milk feta cheese, crumbled
- 2 crushed cloves garlic
- 1/3 cup extra virgin olive oil, plus extra to drizzle
- 100g baby spinach, and more to serve
- 1/4 cup tarragon leaves, chopped
- 2 tbsp. chopped flat-leaf parsley

Directions

Add 1 tablespoon of the oil to a frying pan set over medium heat. Stir in garlic, leeks, and garlic and sauté for about 15 minutes or until leeks are tender. Stir in spinach for about 30 seconds or until wilted. Season with salt and pepper

In a bowl, whisk together 1 tablespoon water, eggs and parsley.

Add 1 tablespoon oil to another pan set over medium high heat; add half of the egg mixture and cook until almost set, for about 2 minutes.

MANAGE YOUR MICROBIOMES

Spoon half of the leek mixture over half of the omelet and fold to enclose. Slide the omelet onto a serving plate and sprinkle with half each of extra spinach and cheese.

Repeat the procedure with remaining olive oil, leek mixture, egg mixture, spinach and cheese.

To serve, drizzle each omelet with more olive oil and sprinkle with pine nuts.

Coconut & Almond Pancakes with Spiced Plums

These super fluffy pancakes are gluten-free and packed with vital vitamins and minerals. Almond flour is fantastic for calming your gut.

Yields: 4 Servings

Total Time: 25 Minutes

Prep Time: 15 Minutes

Cook Time: 10 Minutes

Ingredients

For the plums:

- 12 ripe plums
- 2 tbsp. freshly squeezed orange juice
- 1 tsp. grated orange zest
- 1 tsp. mixed spice
- 1 tbsp. runny honey

For the pancakes:

- 2 tbsp. coconut oil
- 25g coconut flour
- 100g ground almonds
- 200ml coconut milk
- 4 organic free-range eggs
- 1½ tsp. baking-powder
- seeds from 1 vanilla pod
- 1 tsp. ground cinnamon
- 1 tbsp. runny honey

MANAGE YOUR MICROBIOMES

Directions

Preheat your oven to 400°F.

Half the plums, discarding stones, arrange 16 halves cut-side up on a baking sheet lined with parchment paper.

In a bowl, mix orange juice, zest, mixed spice and honey; pour over the plums and roast in the oven for about 15 minutes. Let cool.

In the meantime, blend the remaining plums; set aside.

Add ground almonds in a bowl and sift in cinnamon, coconut flour and baking powder.

Whisk together coconut milk, eggs, honey and vanilla seeds in a separate bowl; beat into the dry ingredients until smooth.

Add a small amount of coconut oil to a frying pan set over low heat; drop in a spoonful of batter and cook for 1 minute. Flip over and cook for 1 minute more. Transfer to a plate and cook the remaining pancakes with the remaining oil.

Gently reheat the plums and serve with the pancakes drizzled with plum sauce.

Green Smoothie

This green smoothie is creamy, delicious and will keep you satisfied throughout the day. It gets a tropical flavor thanks to the addition of coconut water and an extra nutritional boost from spinach.

Yields: 2 Servings

Total Time: 5 Minutes

Prep Time: 5 Minutes

Cook Time: 0 Minutes

Ingredients

- ½ organic cucumber, chopped
- 1 cup coconut water
- 2 cups organic spinach
- ½ avocado, pitted, peeled
- ½ lemon, peeled
- ¼ cup parsley
- 6 ice cubes

Directions

Blend together all ingredients until very smooth. Enjoy!

MANAGE YOUR MICROBIOMES

Amazing Veggie Frittata

This traditional Italian omelet tastes great with just about any combination of herbs; try dill, parsley, marjoram or chervil.

Yields: 4 Servings

Total Time: 40 Minutes

Prep Time: 15 Minutes

Cook Time: 25 Minutes

Ingredients

- 6 organic eggs
- 2 garlic cloves, thinly sliced
- 3-4 cups diced zucchini
- 1 medium sized onion, thinly sliced
- ½ cup coconut milk
- Sea salt
- ¼ cup fresh herbs (parsley, basil, or chives), chopped

Directions

Set an oven-proof pan over medium high heat. Add coconut oil and heat until melted; stir in onions and zucchini and cook until tender. Stir in garlic and continue cooking until fragrant and golden.

In the meantime, beat together eggs, chopped herbs, coconut milk and sea salt.

Add the egg mixture to the pan and transfer to the oven; bake until the center is set, for about 25 minutes.

Serve warm with mixed salad greens.

Microbiome Lunch Recipes

Fennel Cucumber Salad

This unique veggie salad is great when served cold or hot for casual summer lunches or picnics.

Yield: 8 Servings

Total Time: 20 Minutes

Prep Time: 20 Minutes

Cook Time: 0 Minutes

Ingredients

- 3 tbsp. extra virgin olive oil
- 3 tbsp. freshly squeezed lemon juice
- 1 small fennel bulb, sliced
- 1 medium sweet onion, sliced
- 3 large cucumbers, sliced
- 3/4 tsp. dill weed
- 1/4 tsp. lemon zest
- 1/2 tsp. kosher salt
- 1/4 tsp. pepper

Directions

Combine together fennel, cucumber, and onion in a large bowl.

Combine together the remaining ingredients in a jar; seal with a tight-fitting lid and shake well. Pour the dressing over the salad and toss until well coated. Refrigerate until chilled.

Classic Chicken Soup

There's nothing more comforting in cold weather —and flu and cold season —than this classic chicken soup. It is packed with classic flavors and is very gut friendly.

Yields: 2 Servings

Total Time: 1 Hour 5 Minutes

Prep Time: 15 Minutes

Cook Time: 50 Minutes

Ingredients

- 1 3 1/2- to 4-pound chicken
- 1 large yellow onion, quartered
- 4 celery stalks
- 6 carrots, peeled
- 1 tsp. whole black peppercorns
- 2 1/2tsp. kosher salt

Directions

Place chicken in a pot. Cut 2 celery stalks into small pieces and chop 3 carrots into small slices. Chop the onion; add the cut veggies to the pot along with enough water, peppercorns and salt. Bring the mixture to a gentle boil; reduce heat and simmer for about 30 minutes or until chicken is cooked through.

Transfer the cooked chicken to a large bowl and let cool. With a strainer, strain the broth and discard the veggies. Return the broth to the pot. Slice the remaining celery and carrots and add to the pot. Simmer for about 10 minutes. Shred the chicken and add to the pot; simmer for 5 minutes more and serve.

Beer-Steamed Mussels

Garlic, thyme and tarragon lend this healthy mussels a unique flavor that even picky eaters will fall in love with.

Yields: 1 Serving

Total Time: 36 Minutes

Prep Time: 20 Minutes

Cook Time: 16 Minutes

Ingredients

- 1 lb. mussels in shells
- 1 tbsp. olive oil
- 1 tbsp. chopped fresh tarragon
- 1/2 cup gluten-free beer
- 1 large shallot, chopped
- 2 garlic cloves, minced
- 4 sprigs of thyme
- 1/2 tsp. Dijon mustard

Directions

Rinse mussels and tap to close opened mussels, discarding the broken and widely opened ones.

Add extra virgin olive oil to the soup pot; stir in shallots, garlic, thyme, salt and pepper; cook for about 3 minutes. Stir in beer and bring to a gentle boil for about 3 minutes. Add the mussels and steam, covered, for about 10 minutes or until the mussels open.

Smoked Salmon & Asparagus Bundles

Salmon is rich in moega-3 fatty acids, which play an important role in keeping blood from clotting and protecting against irregular heartbeats thus preventing heart attacks. This recipe provides the best way to add this super food to your weekly diet.

Yields: 4 to 6 Servings

Total Time: 30 Minutes

Prep Time: 20 Minutes

Cook Time: 10 Minutes

Ingredients

- 1 bunch asparagus, ends trimmed (about 20 spears)
- 6 ounces smoked salmon, thinly sliced, 1 slice per spear
- 1 tbsp. rosemary, chopped
- 2 tbsp. extra virgin olive oil
- 1/8 tsp. sea salt
- 1/8 tsp. pepper

Directions

Preheat your oven to 400°F.

Arrange asparagus on a baking sheet lined with a foil and drizzle with extra virgin olive oil.

Sprinkle with salt, rosemary and pepper and roast for about 10 minutes or until the edges are browned. Transfer the roasted asparagus to another baking sheet to cool. Wrap each asparagus spear in a smoked salmon slice and serve in a platter.

Healthy Greek Salad with Sheep's Milk Feta

This tasty salad combines great flavors of olives, cucumber, and feta cheese. It replaces high-fat, low-nutrition picnic salads in your household.

Yields: 1 Serving

Total Time: 15 Minutes

Prep Time: 15 Minutes

Cook Time: 0 Minutes

Ingredients

- ¼ peeled cucumber, cubed
- 8 kalamata olives
- 1 medium tomato, sliced
- 2 cups romaine lettuce, roughly chopped
- 1/8 cup sheep's milk feta cheese, crumbled
- 2 tbsp. lemon vinaigrette (see recipe below)
- 1/8 tsp. dried oregano
- 2 thin slices red onion
- ¼ green pepper, sliced
- ¼ sweet red pepper, sliced
- Salt and pepper to taste
- ¼ lemon

Directions

Mix together onion, green peppers, cucumber, olives, tomato and lettuce in a bowl.

In a separate bowl, combine vinaigrette, oregano, salt and pepper.

Serve the veggie mixture on a plate and top with feta crumbles.

Serve drizzled with vinaigrette and garnished with a lemon wedge.

Lemon Vinaigrette

Ingredients

- 2 tbsp. fresh lemon juice
- 1/2 cup extra virgin olive oil
- 1 clove garlic, minced
- 1 tsp. dried oregano
- 2 tbsp. Dijon mustard
- 1/4 cup red wine vinegar
- 1/4 tsp. ground black pepper
- 1/2 tsp. kosher salt

Directions

In a small bowl, whisk together garlic, oregano, Dijon mustard, red wine vinegar, salt and pepper. Gently whisk in extra virgin olive oil until well blended. Beat in lemon juice until well combined and store in a sealable jar.

Mango Salad with Citrus Vinaigrette

This salad is a diabetes-friendly recipe that is worthy trying. It's low in calories and very healthy.

Yield: 1 Serving

Total Time: 15 Minutes

Prep Time: 15 Minutes

Cook Time: 0 Minutes

Ingredients

- Chicken slices
- ¼ red onion, thinly sliced
- 1/2 small avocado, peeled and sliced
- 1/2 small mango, peeled and sliced
- 2 cups arugula leaves

Directions

Toss together arugula and half vinaigrette. Add onion, mango, avocado, salt and pepper; mix until well combined.

Add the chicken and drizzle salad with the remaining vinaigrette. Enjoy!

Steamed Quinoa

Yield: 1 Serving

Total Time: 25 Minutes

Prep Time: 15 Minutes

Cook Time: 10 Minutes

Ingredients

- ¼ cup quinoa, rinsed, drained
- 1 tsp. coconut oil
- ½ cup water
- 1 tsp. chopped parsley
- ½ tsp. chopped thyme
- 1/8 tsp. sea salt
- 1/8 tsp. black pepper

Directions

Melt coconut oil in a saucepan set over medium low heat. Stir in quinoa and toast for about 2 minutes.

Add water and cook for about 8 minutes over low heat until tender. Add thyme, parsley, salt and pepper.

Green Apple, Carrot & Jicama Slaw

The lightness of jicama and apples paired with citric juice makes this slaw extremely refreshing. Delicious!

Yields: 2 Servings

Total Time: 30 Minutes

Prep Time: 30 Minutes

Cook Time: 0 Minutes

Ingredients

- 1 firm pear, shredded
- 2 large carrots, shredded
- 2 cups shredded cabbage
- 2 peeled, cored and shredded apples
- 2 cups shredded radish
- 1 pound jicama, peeled and shredded
- 1 tbsp. freshly squeezed lime juice
- 3 tbsp. freshly squeezed orange juice
- 2 tbsp. extra virgin olive oil
- 1/4 cup finely chopped cilantro
- Sea salt and pepper

Directions

In a mixing bowl, combine pear, carrot, apple, radish, jicama, cabbage, and cilantro; sprinkle with lime juice, orange juice, extra virgin olive oil, salt and pepper. Toss until well combined and serve.

Leek, Courgette and Spinach Quiche

This recipe makes a very versatile and delicious lunch meal for the whole family to enjoy. A green dream!

Yields: 8 Servings

Total Time: 50 Minutes

Prep Time: 20 Minutes

Cook Time: 30 Minutes

Ingredients

- 1 medium courgette, chopped
- 250g sheep's milk feta cheese
- 3 large free-range eggs
- 1 tbsp. extra virgin olive oil
- 1 leek, chopped
- 1 pound fresh spinach
- 1 red onion, chopped
- Sea salt and pepper

Directions

Preheat your oven to 375°F.

Add water to a medium pan and bring to a boil; add spinach and boil for 2 minutes; drain.

Add olive oil to a pan set over medium high heat; add courgette, red onion and chopped leek. Cook for about 4 minutes or until tender.

In a bowl, beat the eggs - add spinach and leek mixture. Add cheese and mix well.

Pour the egg mixture in a baking tin and cook the top is browned. Serve hot or cold with green salad.

Healthy Chicken Salad

If you are a fan of chicken salads, you're going to fall in love with this healthy chicken salad.

Yields: 2 Servings

Total Time: 10 Minutes

Prep Time: 10 Minutes

Cook Time: 0 Minutes

Ingredients

- 8 ounces chicken breast, cooked, cubed
- 1 tbsp. curry powder
- 1 tbsp. mayonnaise
- 1/4 cup nonfat plain yogurt
- 1 tbsp. almonds, toasted
- 1 tbsp. dried cranberries
- 1 stalk celery, finely diced
- 1/2 ripe firm pear, diced
- 1/2 cup sprouts

Directions

In a large bowl, mix together mayonnaise, curry powder and yogurt. Stir in chicken, almonds, cranberries, celery, and pear; toss until combined.

Serve the chicken salad with sprouts.

MANAGE YOUR MICROBIOMES

Greek Tuna Bread

Try this Greek-style version if you're tired of the same old tuna sandwich. Delicious!

Yields: 1 Serving

Total Time: 15 Minutes

Prep Time: 10 Minutes

Cook Time: 5 Minutes

Ingredients

- ¼ cup chopped artichoke hearts, marinated
- 1 plum tomato, chopped
- 2.5 ounces tuna, drained
- 1 tsp. canola oil
- 1 tsp. lemon juice
- 1 tsp. capers, rinsed and chopped
- 1 ounce kalamata olives, pitted, chopped
- 1 minced red onion
- ¼ cup sheep's milk feta cheese, crumbled
- 2 slices gluten-free bread
- Pepper

Directions

In a bowl, flake tuna with a fork; stir in capers, olives, onion, artichokes, feta, tomato, pepper and lemon juice until well blended. Place the mixture over one bread slice and top with the remaining slice.

Add canola oil to a skillet set over medium heat. Put bread sandwich in the skillet and cover; cook for about 2 minutes or until golden on the bottom side. Flip over, reduce heat and cook for 3 more minutes or until the second side is also golden.

Chicken & Veggie Stew

You'll be surprised with the ease with which this amazingly delicious stew is made. It's great for a weekend lunch.

Yields: 4 Servings

Total Time: 9 Hour 35 Minutes

Prep Time: 20 Minutes

Cook Time: 9 Hour 15 Minutes

Ingredients:

- 3-4lb organic chicken
- 1/4 bundle Kale
- 1 tomato
- 8 oz. mushrooms
- 2 cups chopped cabbage
- 1 squash
- 1 lb. carrots
- 1 yellow bell pepper
- 1 green bell pepper
- 1 sweet potato
- 1 large onion
- Salt, pepper, oregano and sage to taste

Directions

Put the chicken in the center of if the crockpot and place the chopped veggies around it. Add 2 cups water and season with salt, pepper, oregano and sage. Cover and cook on low for about 9 hours. 5 minutes before serving, uncover and top with kale. Cook until kale is just wilted and serve.

MANAGE YOUR MICROBIOMES

Strawberry Spinach Salad

Strawberry and spinach salad was a hit in 80's, but this version will amaze you with its refinements! The salad is not sweet, just aromatic and berries provide bursts of fruitiness –it's a perfect addition to any spring party.

Yields: 4 Servings

Total Time: 30 Minutes

Prep Time: 30 Minutes

Cook Time: 0 Minutes

Ingredients

- 1 quart hulled and sliced strawberries
- 10 ounces fresh spinach – chopped
- 1 tbsp. minced onion
- 1 tbsp. poppy seeds
- 2 tbsp. sesame seeds
- 1/4 tsp. Worcestershire sauce
- 1/4 tsp. paprika
- 1/4 cup distilled white vinegar
- 1/2 cup extra virgin olive oil
- 1 tbsp. raw honey
- 1/4 cup silvered almonds, blanched

Directions

In a bowl, whisk together extra virgin olive oil, poppy seeds, honey, sesame seeds, onion, Worcestershire sauce, paprika and vinegar; cover and chill for at least 1 hour.

In a separate bowl, combine almonds, strawberries and spinach; pour the chilled dressing over the salad and toss until well coated; chill for about 10 minutes before serving.

MANAGE YOUR MICROBIOMES

Chickpea Salad

This recipe is so easy, but tastes so FAB! You'll love it!

Yields: 2 Servings

Total Time: 25 Minutes

Prep Time: 20 Minutes

Cook Time: 5 Minutes

Ingredients

- 1 tbsp. lemon juice
- 1 tbsp. mashed avocado
- ½ onion, diced
- 1 clove garlic, minced
- 1 stalk celery, diced
- 15.5 ounces chickpeas
- 1 tsp. dried dill
- Salt
- Pepper

Directions

Sauté onion and garlic in a pan set over medium heat until translucent.

Mash chickpeas in a small bowl until smooth. Add sautéed onion, celery, mashed avocado, lemon juice and dill; stir until well combined.

Season with ground pepper and salt to taste.

Spinach and Beet Salad

Apple cider vinegar is the key to this flavorful and healthy lunch meal. It's delicious!

Yields: 4 Servings

Total Time: 17 Minutes

Prep Time: 10 Minutes

Cook Time: 7 Minutes

Ingredients

- 1 tbsp. extra-virgin olive oil
- 2 cups beet wedges, steamed
- 8 cups baby spinach
- 2 tbsp. sliced Kalamata olives
- 2 plum tomatoes, chopped
- 1 clove garlic, minced
- 1 cup thinly sliced red onion
- 2 tbsp. chopped fresh parsley
- 1/4 tsp. pepper
- 1/4 tsp. salt
- 2 tbsp. apple cider vinegar

Directions

Put spinach in a bowl.

Add oil to a skillet set over medium heat; add onion and sauté, stirring, for about 2 minutes or until tender. Stir in garlic, parsley, olives and tomatoes and cook, stirring for about 3 minutes or until tomatoes break down. Stir in vinegar, beets, salt and pepper and continue cooking for 1 more minute or until the beets are heated through. Toss together spinach and beet mixture until well blended. Serve warm.

MANAGE YOUR MICROBIOMES

Citrus and Spinach Salad

A great, refreshing twist on the basic spinach salad –a perfect complement to any holiday lunch meal.

Yields: 4 Servings

Total Time: 20 Minutes

Prep Time: 20 Minutes

Cook Time: 0 Minutes

Ingredients

- 2 tbsp. freshly squeezed orange or grapefruit juice
- 1 tsp. poppy seeds
- 8 cups chopped spinach
- 1 clove garlic, very finely chopped
- 1/2 small red onion, thinly sliced
- 1/2 tsp. honey
- 1/2 tbsp. Dijon mustard
- 1 tbsp. extra-virgin olive oil
- 1 tbsp. white-wine vinegar
- 1/4 tsp. salt
- Pepper

Directions

Soak onion in a bowl of water for at least 10 minutes; drain and set aside.

In a salad bowl, combine orange (grapefruit) juice, garlic, honey, mustard, extra virgin olive oil, vinegar, salt and pepper; stir in onion, spinach and fruit sections. Serve garnished with poppy seeds.

Avocado & Quinoa Salad

This recipe features a quartet of super foods –quinoa, kale, avocado, and olive oil – that makes it a terrific idea for a super healthy lunch.

Yields: 4 Servings

Total Time: 30 Minutes

Prep Time: 30 Minutes

Cook Time: 0 Minutes

Ingredients

- 1/3 cup red quinoa
- 1 avocado, peeled, sliced
- 2 cups baby spinach leaves
- 1/2 tsp. ground cumin seed
- 2 tbsp. lime juice
- 1/4 cup diced red onion
- 1/2 cup diced cucumber
- 1 cup cherry tomatoes, halved
- 2/3 cup water
- Salt
- Pepper

Directions

Spread cooked quinoa into a bowl and refrigerate until chilled.

Remove from the refrigerator and stir in onion, cucumber and tomatoes. Season the mixture with salt, pepper, cumin, and lime juice. Divide spinach onto serving plates and top each with quinoa salad. To serve, garnish with avocado slices.

Cucumber & Arugula Salad with Lemon Dressing

This is a gut friendly salad made with just five ingredients –arugula, cucumber, extra virgin olive oil, lemon juice, and salt. It tastes great.

Yields: 2 Servings

Total Time: 5 Minutes

Prep Time: 5 Minutes

Cook Time: 0 Minutes

Ingredients

- 2 tbsp. extra virgin olive oil
- 3 medium cucumbers, sliced
- 1 tbsp. lemon juice
- 5 ounces arugula
- ⅛ tsp. sea salt

Directions

In a large bowl, combine together all ingredients and serve.

Grapefruit-Kale Salad

Loads of kale and grapefruit make this salad substantial, hearty and loaded with fiber. It's simple and fast (and of course healthy) – perfect anytime of the year.

Yields: 2 Servings

Total Time: 25 Minutes

Prep Time: 25 Minutes

Cook Time: 0 Minutes

Ingredients

- 1 tbsp. extra virgin olive oil
- 1 bunch kale, sliced into small ribbons
- 1 grapefruit, chopped
- 1 tsp. apple cider vinegar
- ⅛ tsp. sea salt
- Juice of 1 lime

Directions

Drizzle kale with extra virgin olive oil and massage with hands to coat well.

Sprinkle with salt, vinegar and lime juice. Add the grapefruit and toss well.

Let sit for at least 15 minutes before serving.

MANAGE YOUR MICROBIOMES

Almond Chicken Salad

Nothing beat the tasty combo of chicken, almonds and cranberries. This recipe serves great as a healthy potluck or luncheon dish.

Yields: 6 to 8 Servings

Total Time: 30 Minutes

Prep Time: 20 Minutes

Cook Time: 10 Minutes

Ingredients

- ½ cup extra virgin olive oil
- 2 cups chicken, shredded
- 4 cups fresh greens
- 3 apples, sliced and chopped
- 1 cup dried cranberries
- 1 cup slivered almonds, blanched, toasted
- ¼ cup apple cider vinegar
- ¼ tsp. sea salt

Directions

Toast the almonds in a pan set over low heat until lightly browned.

In the meantime, core and chop the apples.

Toss together warm almonds, chicken, chopped apples, cranberries and greens in a large bowl.

Drizzle the salad with vinegar and extra virgin olive oil; sprinkle with salt to serve.

Healthy Curried Shrimp

This exceedingly scrumptious and easy-to-cook shrimp dish is a healthy alternative to meat and fish -perfect for a weekend lunch.

Yields: 4 to 6 Servings

Total Time: 45 Minutes

Prep Time: 20 Minutes

Cook Time: 25 Minutes

Ingredients

- 4 tbsp. extra virgin olive oil
- 3 tbsp. freshly squeezed lime juice
- 1 pound shrimp, peeled
- 1 bunch cilantro, chopped
- ½ tsp. turmeric
- ½ tsp. coriander
- ½ tsp. cumin
- 2 tsp. fresh ginger, minced
- ½ cup tomatoes, pureed
- 1 medium onion, chopped
- 4 cloves garlic

Directions

Heat oil in a saucepan set over medium heat; add onion and garlic and sauté for about 10 minutes or until tender.

Stir in coriander, cumin, ginger, tomatoes and turmeric and simmer for about 5 minutes. Add shrimp to the sauce and continue cooking for about 10 minutes.

Stir in cilantro and remove the pan from heat.

Stir in lime juice to serve.

Microbiome Diet Dinner Recipes

Roasted Asparagus w/ Lemon Vinaigrette
Roasting intensifies the sweetness in the microbiome super food – asparagus. This is a healthy and delicious dinner dish that will be loved by everyone.

Yield: 4 Servings

Total Time: 20 Minutes

Prep Time: 10 Minutes

Cook Time: 10 Minutes

Ingredients

- 2 tbsp. extra-virgin olive oil
- 3/4 pound fresh asparagus
- Pinch kosher salt
- Pinch black pepper

For the Vinaigrette:

- 1 tbsp. extra virgin olive oil
- 1/2 lemon, juiced
- 1/2 tsp. Dijon mustard
- Black pepper
- Kosher salt

Directions

Preheat your oven to 400°F.

Toss together asparagus, extra virgin olive oil, salt and pepper in a bowl. Spread the asparagus on a baking sheet and roast for about 10 minutes or until tender.

In the meantime, make the vinaigrette: whisk together lemon juice and mustard in a bowl. Whisk in olive oil, salt and pepper.

Serve the asparagus on a plate and toss with vinaigrette.

Garlic and Chickpea Soup

Irresistible aromas emerge from this garlicky soup that has been brewing without as much as a stir. This hearty soup is loaded with veggies and chickpeas -it is a meal all in itself.

Yield: 4 Servings

Total Time: 55 Minutes

Prep Time: 15 Minutes

Cook Time: 40 Minutes

Ingredients

- 6 tbsp. extra virgin olive oil, divided
- 4 cups homemade vegetable broth
- 15 ounce chickpeas
- 1/2 tsp. red pepper flakes
- 1 tbsp. minced thyme
- 8 cloves garlic, thinly sliced
- Apple cider vinegar
- Kosher salt

Directions

In a sauté pan, combine garlic, 3 tablespoons extra virgin olive oil, pepper flakes and thyme; cook over medium heat, stirring, for about 5 minutes or until fragrant. Stir in chickpeas and continue cooking for 2 minutes more. Add broth and bring the mixture to a boil. Lower heat and simmer for about 30 minutes.

Stir in the remaining oil and blend in a blender until very smooth. Season the soup with apple cider vinegar and salt; ladle into serving bowls and serve.

Colorful Veggie Detox Salad

Detox your week away with this raw veggie salad. It's rich in vitamin A and C and fiber.

Ingredients

- 1/2 cup tahini dressing (recipe below)
- 2 julienned medium carrots
- 1 small head romaine lettuce, grated
- 1 small head purple cabbage, grated

For Dressing:

- 2 tbsp. extra virgin olive oil
- 1/2 cup freshly squeezed lemon juice
- 1/2 cup raw tahini
- 1 tsp. sea salt

Directions

Puree together the roasted tahini, extra virgin olive oil, lemon juice, and sea salt until smooth; set aside half cup for salad and store the rest.

In a bowl, combine together carrots, lettuce, cabbage; toss with the dressing and serve.

Silky Cauliflower Soup

This simple and elegant soup has body and tang thanks to addition of coconut milk and herbs. It's creamy, hearty and very healthy.

Yield: 4 Servings

Total Time: 45 Minutes

Prep Time: 15 Minutes

Cook Time: 30 Minutes

Ingredients

- 3 tsp. extra virgin olive oil
- 1/2 cup chopped leeks
- 1 1/4 cups chopped green cabbage
- 1 1/2 pounds chopped cauliflower
- 2 1/2 cups celery juice
- 2 cups coconut milk
- 3/4 tsp. thyme leaves
- 1 1/2 tsp. minced rosemary
- 1/2 cup chopped parsnip
- 2 tbsp. minced garlic
- Nutmeg
- 1 tsp. kosher salt
- Black pepper

Directions

Add oil to a stockpot; sauté leeks, cauliflower, garlic, parsnips, thyme and rosemary until cauliflower is browned.

Stir in coconut milk and celery juice and simmer for about 30 minutes. Stir in nutmeg, salt and pepper and blend with an immersion blender until smooth.

Cucumber Kimchi

Cucumber kimchi is a popular dish enjoyed in the summer. It's a perfect example of the ying and the yang in Korean cuisine. The spiciness of chili powder is balanced with the coolness of the cucumbers.

Yields: 6 Servings

Total Time: 40 Minutes

Prep Time: 40 Minutes

Cook Time: 0 Minutes

Ingredients

- 2 pickling cucumbers (8 ounces)
- 2 tbsp. apple cider vinegar
- 1 1/4-inch piece ginger, finely chopped
- 2 scallions, finely chopped
- 2 cloves garlic, finely chopped
- 1 tsp. kosher salt
- 1 tbsp. Korean chile powder
- 1/2 tsp. fish sauce

Directions

Half the cucumbers lengthwise and then crosswise into small half-moons; transfer to a bowl and combine with salt. Let stand for about 30 minutes.

In the meantime, combine vinegar, chile powder, ginger, scallions, garlic, and fish sauce in a bowl.

Drain the cucumbers, discarding the liquid and stir into the vinegar mixture.

Refrigerate for at least 12 hours before serving.

MANAGE YOUR MICROBIOMES

Goat Cheese Asparagus Soufflés

Warm and puffy, these asparagus soufflés are the essence of spring. They are great when served with a bowl of green salad with tangy vinaigrette.

Yield: 6 Servings

Total Time: 50 Minutes

Prep Time: 20 Minutes

Cook Time: 30 Minutes

Ingredients

- 1 pound asparagus, trimmed
- 1 cup diced or crumbled goat cheese
- 8 large egg whites
- 4 large egg yolks
- 3 tbsp. gluten-free flour
- 2 tbsp. coconut oil
- 1 1/2 cups coconut milk
- Pinch of ground nutmeg
- 1/2 tsp. kosher salt, divided
- 1/4 tsp. freshly ground pepper

Directions

Add 3 cups water to a skillet and bring to a gentle boil. Add asparagus and cook, partially covered, for about 3 minutes or until tender-crisp. Drain and rinse under cold water; blot dry with a kitchen towel and cut into small slices.

Place rack on the lowest oven level and preheat to 375°F.

Grease ramekins with olive oil cooking spray and place them on a rimmed baking sheet.

Set a skillet over medium heat; add milk and heat until hot.

In a saucepan, melt coconut oil and whisk in flour. Cook for about 2 minutes and turn off heat. Gently whisk in milk and return the heat to medium low. Cook, whisking for 4 minutes more or until thickened. Whisk in ¼ teaspoon each of nutmeg, salt and pepper and remove from heat.

Whisk in four egg yolks, one at a time and transfer the mixture to a bowl. Stir in goat cheese and asparagus.

Beat eight egg whites in a bowl with an electric mixer until foam is formed. Stir in the remaining salt, nutmeg and pepper until well combined.

Gently fold egg whites into egg yolk until well blended. Divide the mixture among ramekins, not filling them to the top; bake for about 25 minutes at 145°F.

Liver and Onions

Craving for liver? Try out this easy skillet meal that will be on your table in just 25 minutes.

Yield: 4 Servings

Total Time: 25 Minutes

Prep Time: 15 Minutes

Cook Time: 10 Minutes

Ingredients

- 2 tbsp. extra virgin olive oil
- 5 large onions, sliced
- 4 large slices beef liver
- Salt
- Pepper

Directions

Add olive oil to a skillet set over medium low heat; sauté onions until tender and caramelized.

Place liver to a separate pan set over medium high heat and cook for about 3 minutes per side or until cooked through.

Top the liver with the caramelized onions and homemade salsa.

Pesto Tilapia

This fish is flaky, tender and so moist with that tasty pesto on top. This recipe makes the perfect light meal that will keep your waistline ready for a bathing suit.

Yield: 4 Servings

Total Time: 45 Minutes

Prep Time: 15 Minutes

Cook Time: 30 Minutes

Ingredients

- 1/2 cup homemade pesto
- 2 tilapia filets

Directions

Preheat your oven to 400°F.

Drizzle each fillet with pesto and place in a greased baking dish; bake for about 30 minutes. Serve over quinoa.

MANAGE YOUR MICROBIOMES

Turkey Chili

Comfort food at its finest —enjoy this hearty nutritious turkey chili that is packed with great flavors —you can't get enough!

Yield: 4 Servings

Total Time: 55 Minutes

Prep Time: 15 Minutes

Cook Time: 40 Minutes

Ingredients

- 3 to 4 cups turkey meat, cooked, shredded
- 1 tbsp. extra virgin olive oil
- 1 cup chicken or turkey stock
- 4 garlic cloves, minced
- 2 tbsp. tomato paste
- 2 cups diced tomatoes
- 2 bell pepper, chopped
- 2 cups onions, chopped
- 2 cups carrots, sliced
- 1 tsp. dried oregano
- 1 tbsp. red pepper flakes
- 1 tbsp. ground cumin
- 2 tbsp. chili powder
- Sea salt
- Pepper
- Green onions, sliced, for garnishing

Directions

Heat extra virgin olive oil in a large skillet set over medium heat; add onion and sauté for about 5 minutes or until golden. Stir in garlic, red pepper flakes, cumin, chili powder and oregano for about 1 minute.

Add tomatoes, tomato paste, turkey and turkey stock and season to taste.

Bring the mixture to a gentle boil; lower heat and simmer for about 30 minutes.

Serve garnished with sliced green onions.

Roasted Garlic Cabbage

Roasted cabbage tastes amazing especially when roasted in this healthy way.

It is SO simple and easy to make.

Yield: 4 Servings

Total Time: 55 Minutes

Prep Time: 15 Minutes

Cook Time: 40 Minutes

Ingredients

- 3 tbsp. extra-virgin olive oil
- 1 big green cabbage, sliced
- 5 garlic cloves, minced
- Sea salt
- Pepper

Directions

Preheat your oven to 400°F.

Brush the cabbage with extra virgin olive oil and spread evenly with garlic; season with salt and pepper and roast in the oven for about 20 minutes.

Turn the cabbage slices over and continue roasting for 20 more minutes or until crispy.

Roasted Sage and Lemon Chicken

This is one of the best roasted chicken dishes with incredible flavors that will please even the pickiest eater. It pairs well with seasonal veggies.

Yield: 4 Servings

Total Time: 45 Minutes

Prep Time: 15 Minutes

Cook Time: 30 Minutes

Ingredients

- 1 1/2 lb. chicken breast
- 2 tbsp. extra virgin olive oil
- 1 bunch fresh sage, chopped
- 1 lemon sliced
- Sea salt
- Pepper

Directions

Preheat your oven to 450°F.

Make a pocket between the meat and skin; spread extra virgin olive oil under the skin, then add sage, lemon slices, salt and pepper.

Rub outside of the chicken with extra virgin olive oil, salt and pepper and place it on the rack; roast in the oven for about 30 minutes or until golden brown.

Eggplant Chicken Stew

The amazing flavors of the Mediterranean –tomatoes, chives, extra virgin olive oil, and eggplant –are captured in this delicious and savory stew.

Yield: 3 Servings

Total Time: 30 Minutes

Prep Time: 15 Minutes

Cook Time: 15 Minutes

Ingredients

- 1 chicken breast
- 2 cups chopped kale
- 2 cups chopped spinach
- 1 tbsp. extra-virgin olive oil
- 2 tbsp. chopped fresh chives
- 1 medium-sized eggplant, cubed
- ½ tsp. smoked paprika
- 1 tbsp. dried basil
- 1 15 oz. diced tomatoes
- Sea salt
- Pepper
- Crushed red pepper

Directions

Heat extra virgin olive oil in a pan set over medium heat. Add eggplant and chives and sauté for about 5 minutes or until eggplant is tender.

Chop the cooked chicken into cubes and add to the pan with eggplant. Cook for about 7 minutes or until chicken is cooked through.

Stir in kale and spinach until wilted.

Serve warm.

Crock Pot Chili

This is a perfect example of a recipe that is passed down from generation to generation. This is the meal you want to prepare on a special night.

Ingredients

- 1 pound cooked ground beef
- 1 large onion, chopped
- 2 rib celery, chopped
- 1 cup chopped green pepper
- 64 ounces tomato juice
- 32 – 40 ounces chopped tomatoes
- Crushed red pepper
- 1 tsp. pepper
- 1 tbsp. cumin
- 3 tbsp. chili powder
- 2 tsp. sea salt

Directions

Combine all ingredients in a crockpot and cook on low heat for about 8 hours.

Garnish with chopped raw onion and avocado and serve with whole-grain muffins.

Shrimp Fried Cauliflower Rice

This hearty fried shrimp recipe replaces rice with cauliflower for a grain free and nutrient dense dinner dish that is healthy, delicious and filling.

Ingredients

- 2 free-range eggs, beaten
- 2 cups cooked cauliflower rice
- 1/4 cup chopped red bell pepper
- 1/2 cup peas
- 1 medium carrot, chopped
- 8 oz. peeled and deveined shrimp
- 2 cloves garlic, minced
- 1 cup chopped onion
- 1 tbsp. coconut oil
- Salt
- Pepper

Directions

Melt coconut oil in a pan set over medium high heat; add garlic and onion and sauté for about 4 minutes or until tender. Stir in shrimp for about 1 minute.

Stir in bell pepper, peas, and carrot and cook for about 4 minutes. Stir in cauliflower rice and make a well in the center of the mixture. Pour the beaten eggs in the well and stir to scramble. Season with salt and pepper to serve.

Chicken with Peppers

This chicken with peppers dish adds Italian flair to your meal in just 45 minutes. It's simple and delicious.

Yield: 4 Servings

Total Time: 45 Minutes

Prep Time: 15 Minutes

Cook Time: 30 Minutes

Ingredients

- 2 tsp. extra virgin olive oil
- 10 ounces chicken breast halves, skinless, boneless, trimmed
- 3 kalamata olives
- ¼ cups tomato, chopped
- ¼ red bell pepper, cut into small strips
- ¼ yellow bell pepper, cut into small strips
- ¼ cups onion, sliced
- Cooking spray
- 1 tsp. oregano, chopped
- ½ tbsp. parsley, chopped
- ¼ tsp. pepper
- ¼ tsp. salt

Directions

In a nonstick skillet, sauté onion in oil over medium high heat for about 5 minutes or until golden brown. Raise heat to high and stir in bell peppers; sauté until peppers are tender, for about 10 minutes. Stir in tomato, black pepper and salt and continue cooking for 7 more minutes or until all liquid has evaporated. Stir in olives, oregano, and parsley and cook for 1 more minute. Transfer the mixture to a bowl and keep warm.

Wipe the pan clean and coat it lightly with cooking spray. Add chicken and cook until done, for about 3 minutes per side. Stir in the tomato mixture and cook until heated through, for about 1 minute.

Warm Lemon Chicken

This warm lemon chicken recipe makes a light and tasty dinner meal, perfect for those who are on diet.

Yield: 4 Servings

Total Time: 50 Minutes

Prep Time: 10 Minutes

Cook Time: 40 Minutes

Ingredients

- 10 ounces chicken thighs, skinless, boneless
- ½ red cabbage, shredded
- 20g baby spinach leaves
- 1 tsp. apple cider vinegar
- 1 carrots, cut into ribbons
- ½ tsp. extra virgin olive oil
- 1 sprig thyme
- Juice and zest from 1/2 lemons
- 1 crushed garlic cloves

Directions

Remove the skin from the chicken and place it between two baking sheets; bash with a meat tenderizer or a rolling pin to flatten.

Place the chicken in a dish and generously season with pepper and salt. Stir in half lemon juice and lemon zest and sprinkle with thyme.

Set a pan or griddle over medium heat and fry the chicken for about 15 minutes or until cooked through and golden brown.

In a bowl, combine carrots, red cabbage and spinach. Divide salad between serving plates and top each with chicken. Drizzle with the remaining lemon juice, vinegar and cooking juices.

Coconut Chicken

Simple, crispy and flavorful chicken using the convenient pantry ingredients to create a wonderful meal everyone will love.

Yield: 2 Servings

Total Time: 45 Minutes

Prep Time: 15 Minutes

Cook Time: 30 Minutes

Ingredients

- 8 ounces chicken breast, boneless, skinless
- ½ tsp. coconut oil
- 3 free-range egg whites
- 1 tsp. sea salt
- 1 tbsp. coconut, shredded
- 1 tbsp. gluten-free flour

Directions

In a bowl, combine shredded coconut, flour and sea salt.

In a separate bowl, beat the egg; dip the chicken in the egg and roll in the flour mixture until well coated.

Add coconut oil to a pan set over medium heat and fry the chicken until the crust begins to brown.

Transfer the chicken to the oven and bake at 350°F for about 10 minutes.

MANAGE YOUR MICROBIOMES

Chicken Bruschetta

The great taste of bruschetta doesn't have to wait for those special occasions. The easy combo of ingredients in this recipe will be the perfect twist to add a bit of jazz back into your typical grilled chicken routine.

Yield: 4 Servings

Total Time: 25 Minutes

Prep Time: 15 Minutes

Cook Time: 10 Minutes

Ingredients

- 10 ounces chicken breasts, skinless, boneless
- ½ tsp. extra virgin olive oil
- 1.8 ounces cherry tomatoes
- 1 tsp. apple cider vinegar
- 0.5 ounces fresh basil leaves
- 1 small cloves garlic, minced
- 1 small onions, chopped

Directions

Add half of the oil to the skillet and cook chicken over medium heat.

In the meantime, slice basil leaves and prepare the veggies.

Heat the remaining oil and sauté garlic and onion for about 3 minutes. Stir in basil and tomatoes for about 5 minutes. Stir in vinegar.

Serve the cooked chicken; cook until heated through and serve topped with onion and tomato mixture.

Fried Salmon Fillets

This crispy, crunchy salmon dish rivals the best roast chicken's tender, moist and flavorful meat that melts in your mouth.

Yield: 2 Servings

Total Time: 35 Minutes

Prep Time: 15 Minutes

Cook Time: 20 Minutes

Ingredients

- 5 ounces tilapia fillet, skin and bones removed
- ¼ tsp. basil
- ¼ tsp. ground paprika
- ¼ tsp. oregano
- ¼ tsp. ground white pepper
- ¼ tsp. thyme
- ¼ tsp. ground black pepper
- 2 tsp. salt
- ¼ tsp. onion powder
- ¼ tsp. ground cayenne pepper
- 2 tsp. extra virgin olive oil
- ¼ cup cooked brown rice, for serving

Directions

Combine oregano, basil, thyme, black pepper, white pepper, salt, onion powder, cayenne pepper, and paprika in a small bowl.

Brush fish with half of oil and sprinkle with the spice mixture. Drizzle with the remaining oil and cook fish in a skillet set over high heat until blackened and flakes easily with a fork. Serve with cooked brown rice.

Zucchini Ribbon Salad

Zucchini ribbons are barely slicked with olive oil and lemon juice to make a great dinner dish. This recipe is simple and easy to make and requires no fancy gadget to get it ready.

Yield: 4 Servings

Total Time: 15 Minutes

Prep Time: 15 Minutes

Cook Time: 0 Minutes

Ingredients

- 300g zucchini
- 2 tbsp. olive oil
- Juice of 1 lemon
- ½ small pack mint, chopped
- ½ small pack chives, chopped

Directions

Combine lemon juice, salt and pepper in a bowl. Whisk in extra virgin olive oil and then stir in the chopped herbs.

Spiralize the zucchini through a spiralizer into the bowl with the dressing. Toss to combine well and serve immediately.

Microbiome Diet Snacks

Roasted Sweet Potato Chips

Seasoned salt and extra virgin olive oil is all you need to turn fresh sweet potatoes into tasty and healthy baked appetizers. These are a low fat and calorie nutritious appetizer. They are perfect for parties.

Yields: 1 to 2 Servings

Total Time: 1 Hour 15 Minutes

Prep Time: 15 Minutes

Cook Time: 1 Hour

Ingredients

- 1 tbsp. extra virgin olive oil
- 1 large sweet potato
- Salt

Directions

Preheat your oven to 300°F.

Scrub potato and slice into thin slices.

Toss together the potato slices with salt and extra virgin olive oil in a bowl; arrange them in a single layer on a cookie sheet. Bake for about 1 hour, flipping every 15 minutes, until crispy and browned.

MANAGE YOUR MICROBIOMES

Roasted Asparagus

Roasting asparagus brings out its inherent woody flavor. This recipe makes a great snack that is gut friendly and very healthy.

Yield: 4 Servings

Total Time: 15 Minutes

Prep Time: 5 Minutes

Cook Time: 10 Minutes

Ingredients

- 1 tbsp. extra virgin olive oil
- 1 pound fresh asparagus
- 1 medium lemon, zested
- 1/2 tsp. freshly grated nutmeg
- 1/2 tsp. kosher salt
- ½ tsp. black pepper

Directions

Preheat your oven to 500°F. Arrange asparagus on an aluminum foil and drizzle with extra virgin olive oil; toss until well coated. Spread the asparagus in a single layer and fold the edges of foil to make a tray. Roast the asparagus in the oven for about 5 minutes; toss and continue roasting for 5 minutes more or until browned. Sprinkle the roasted asparagus with nutmeg, salt, zest and pepper to serve.

Guacamole with Vegetables

Yields: 2 Servings

Total Time: 15 Minutes

Prep Time: 15 Minutes

Cook Time: 0 Minutes

Ingredients

- 2 avocados
- Juice of 1 lime
- Zest of lime
- 1 clove garlic, peeled, minced
- 1/4 red onion, peeled, diced
- Fresh cilantro, chopped
- Sea salt
- Veggies (peppers, celery, cucumber etc.) for serving

Directions

In a bowl, mash together all ingredients to your desired consistency. Garnish with cilantro sprigs and store, covered, in a plastic wrap.

MANAGE YOUR MICROBIOMES

Kale Chips

Extra virgin olive oil, nutritious yeast and salt are all you need to turn the fresh kale into delicious and nutritious snacks. They are crunchy and addictive.

Yields: 6 Servings

Total Time: 35 Minutes

Prep Time: 15 Minutes

Cook Time: 20 Minutes

Ingredients

- 6 ounces kale
- 1 tbsp. extra virgin olive oil
- 2 tbsp. nutritional yeast
- Sea salt

Directions

Preheat your oven to 300°F.

Wash and pat dry kale, and then remove tough center ribs and stems; cut into large pieces.

In a large bowl, toss together the chopped kale with extra virgin olive oil and sea salt; arrange the leaves in a single layer on a baking sheet and bake until crisp, for about 20 minutes. Transfer the baking sheet to rack to cool the kale chips before serving.

Hard-Boiled Eggs with Avocado

Try out this green deviled eggs to reap the health benefits of baked egg in avocado. The perfect healthy snack to enjoy anytime of the day.

Yields: 2 Servings

Total Time: 15 Minutes

Prep Time: 15 Minutes

Cook Time: 0 Minutes

Ingredients

- 1/2 avocado, diced
- 2 hard-boiled free range eggs
- 1 tsp. fresh herbs
- Dash of hot sauce

Directions

Peel the eggs and rinse under cold water. Slice the eggs into quarters and combine with diced avocado in a bowl. Garnish with fresh herbs and hot sauce and enjoy!

MANAGE YOUR MICROBIOMES

Healthy Fried Plantain

These are paleo friendly snacks that you'll fall in love with once you try them. Delicious!

Yields: 2 Servings

Total Time: 28 Minutes

Prep Time: 10 Minutes

Cook Time: 18 Minutes

Ingredients

- 2 very ripe plantains
- 1 tsp. ground cinnamon
- 1/4 cup water
- 3 tbsp. virgin coconut oil

Directions

Cut the peeled plantains in half; again cut the halves into half lengthwise.

Add coconut oil to a pan set over medium high heat; sauté the plantains for about 8 minutes. Turn them over and add enough water to cover; simmer for about 10 minutes or until softened.

Sprinkle with cinnamon and serve warm.

Pickled Veggies

One thing is for sure: these pickled veggies are crisp, tangy, and not intimidating to prepare or eat. You'll love them.

Yields: 16 Servings

Total Time: 17 Minutes

Prep Time: 15 Minutes

Cook Time: 2 Minutes

Ingredients:

- 1 ½ cups green beans, halved
- 2 cups sliced zucchini
- 1 ½ cups sliced onions
- 1 large red pepper, sliced
- 1 tbsp. honey
- 1 tbsp. pickling spice
- 1 cup apple cider vinegar
- Salt

Directions:

Lightly sprinkle salt over onions, beans, zucchini and pepper; let stand for at least 15 minutes. Rinse well and stir into boiling water; cook for about 2 minutes. Drain and rinse with cold water.

Combine pickling spice ad vinegar in a pan; bring to a gentle boil; remove from heat and let cool. Stir in honey and pour over the veggies. You can refrigerate up to 14 days.

Stuffed Celery Bites

What a delicious twist on a favorite snack! It is a simple and easy to make snack to serve guests at a party.

Yields: 8 Servings

Total Time: 19 Minutes

Prep Time: 15 Minutes

Cook Time: 4 Minutes

Ingredients:

- Celery leaves
- 2 tbsp. sunflower seeds, dry-roasted
- 1/4 cup Italian cheese blend, shredded
- 1 (8-ounce) fat-free cream cheese
- 8 stalks celery
- 1 clove garlic, minced
- 2 tbsp. pine nuts
- Olive oil cooking spray

Directions:

Coat a nonstick skillet with olive oil cooking spray; add garlic and pine nuts and sauté over medium heat for about 4 minutes or until the nuts are golden brown. Set aside.

Cut off the wide base and tops from celery and remove 2 thin strips from the round side of celery to create a flat surface.

Combine Italian cheese and cream cheese in a bowl; spread into celery and cut each celery stalk into 2-inch pieces.

Sprinkle half of the celery pieces with sunflower seeds and half with the pine nut mixture; cover and let stand for at least 4 hours before serving.

Pesto-Stuffed Mushrooms

If you're a fan of flavorful mushrooms and pesto and of course all things Italian, then you'll love this pesto-stuffed mushroom recipe. You'll never get enough of it!

Yields: 14 Servings

Total Time: 4 Hours 15 Minutes

Prep Time: 4 Hour 15 Minutes

Cook Time: 0 Minutes

Ingredients:

- 14+ button mushrooms, washed and stemmed
- 1/2 cup extra virgin olive oil
- 3 cloves garlic
- 2 cups basil
- 1/2 cup pine nuts
- 1 cup walnuts
- 1/2 tsp. sea salt

Directions:

Arrange the mushroom caps top-side down on a plate.

In a food processor, blend together stuffing ingredients until very smooth.

Scoop an equal amount of the stuffing into each cap and dehydrate at 105°F until soft, for about 6 hours.

Serve warm.

MANAGE YOUR MICROBIOMES

Healthy Sautéed Kale

This snack is super easy to make and of course super healthy.

Yields: 4 Servings

Total Time: 30 Minutes

Prep Time: 10 Minutes

Cook Time: 20 Minutes

Ingredients

- 1 bunch kale, chopped
- 1 medium onion, chopped
- 2 tbsp. extra virgin olive oil
- ¼ tsp. sea salt

Directions

Heat extra virgin olive oil in a pan set over medium heat. Stir in onion and sauté over medium low heat for about 15 minutes or until caramelized.

Stir in kale and sauté for 5 more minutes. Season with salt to serve.

Vinegar & Salt Kale Chips

Kale seasoned with apple cider vinegar is a deluxe combination. These kale chips are a crowd pleaser!

Yields: 4 Servings

Total Time: 37 Minutes

Prep Time: 25 Minutes

Cook Time: 12 Minutes

Ingredients

- 1 tsp. extra virgin olive oil
- 1 head kale, chopped
- 1 tbsp. apple cider vinegar
- ½ tsp. sea salt

Directions

Place kale in a bowl and drizzle with vinegar and extra virgin olive oil; sprinkle with salt and massage the ingredients with hands.

Spread the kale out onto two paper-lined baking sheets and bake at 375°F for about 12 minutes or until crispy.

Let cool for about 10 minutes before serving.

MANAGE YOUR MICROBIOMES

Squash Fries

These squash fries tastes like potato fries but better. They make a healthy snack to be enjoyed anytime of the day.

Yields: 6 Servings

Total Time: 25 Minutes

Prep Time: 15 Minutes

Cook Time: 10 Minutes

Ingredients

- 1 tbsp. grapeseed oil
- 1 medium butternut squash
- 1/8 tsp. sea salt

Directions

Peel and remove seeds from the squash; cut into thin slices and place them in a bowl. Coat with extra virgin olive oil and grapeseed oil; sprinkle with salt and toss to coat well.

Arrange the squash slices onto three baking sheets and broil in the oven until crispy.

Spinach Cake

Make this delicious spinach cake with those pounds of spinach crowding in the vegetable drawer of your fridge. It's fluffy, moist and irresistible.

Yields: 12 Spinach Cakes

Total Time: 1 Hour Minutes

Prep Time: 15 Minutes

Cook Time: 45 Minutes

Ingredients

- 1 ½ pounds spinach, rinsed
- 2 large eggs, whisked
- 2 cloves garlic, minced
- 1 cup pine nuts
- 3 tbsp. grapeseed oil
- ½ cup currants
- 1 tsp. sea salt

Directions

Wilt spinach in a pan set over low heat for about 5 minutes; drain and let cool a bit before squeezing moisture out of the spinach.

Pulse the spinach in a food processor until coarsely chopped; set aside.

Warm oil in a skillet; add pine nuts and sauté for a few minutes or until golden browned.

Stir in garlic and continue cooking for 1 more minute.

Combine the pine mixture, currants, blended spinach and salt in a bowl; spread the mixture into a coated baking dish and bake at 350°F for about 35 minutes.

Carrot French Fries

Turn carrots into fun fries with a healthier profile by baking then in the oven and serving them fry-style. It is a healthy way to make kids eat veggies.

Yields: 2 Servings

Total Time: 35 Minutes

Prep Time: 15 Minutes

Cook Time: 20 Minutes

Ingredients

- 2 tbsp. extra virgin olive oil
- 6 large carrots
- ½ tsp. sea salt

Directions

Chop the carrots into 2-inch sections and then cut each section into thin sticks.

Toss together the carrots sticks with extra virgin olive oil and salt in a bowl and spread into a baking sheet lined with parchment paper.

Bake the carrot sticks at 425° for about 20 minutes or until browned.

Roasted Balsamic Beets

Roasting the beets in the oven intensifies their sweetness. The tart taste of balsamic vinegar balances the sweetness of the roasted beets to create a delicious snack that everyone will love.

Yields: 4 Servings

Total Time: 1 Hour 30 Minutes

Prep Time: 15 Minutes

Cook Time: 1 Hour 15 Minutes

Ingredients

- 2 tbsp. extra virgin olive oil
- 1 tbsp. balsamic vinegar
- 3-4 medium beets
- ½ tsp. sea salt

Directions

Scrub the beets and wash well; cut into 6 wedges and place them in a baking dish.

Drizzle the beets with extra virgin olive oil, vinegar and salt and bake, covered, at 375°F for about 1 hour. Uncover and continue baking for 15 more minutes or until almost tender.

Candied Macadamia Nuts

These are perfect healthy appetizer, snack or desserts.

Yields: 6 Servings

Total Time: 30 Minutes

Prep Time: 15 Minutes

Cook Time: 15 Minutes

Ingredients

- 2 cups macadamia nuts
- 1 tbsp. extra virgin olive oil
- 2 tbsp. honey
- ½ tsp. sea salt

Directions

In a bowl, toss together all ingredients and spread into a baking dish. Bake at 350°F for about 15 minutes or until browned.

Remove from oven and let cool before serving.

Fig Tapenade

The clever mix of kalamata olives, figs, and olive oil makes this fig tapenade very special and healthy.

Yields: 16 Servings

Total Time: 15 Minutes

Prep Time: 15 Minutes

Cook Time: 0 Minutes

Ingredients

- 1 cup dried figs
- ½ tsp. balsamic vinegar
- 1 tbsp. extra virgin olive oil
- 1 cup kalamata olives
- 1 tbsp. chopped fresh thyme
- ½ cup water

Directions

Pulse the figs in a food processor until well chopped; add water and continue pulsing to form a paste. Add olives and pulse until well blended.

Add thyme, vinegar and extra virgin olive oil and pulse until very smooth. Serve with walnut crackers.

Veggie Snack

This veggie snack is packed with flavor and nutrients. It's gut friendly too.

Yields: 1 Serving

Total Time: 10 Minutes

Prep Time: 10 Minutes

Cook Time: 0 Minutes

Ingredients

- 1 yellow pepper
- 5 stalks celery
- 5 carrots

Directions

Scrub the carrots and rinse under running water.

Rinse celery and yellow pepper; deseed the pepper and chop the veggies into small sticks.

Combine in a bowl and serve.

Guacamole Deviled Eggs

For parties and potlucks, these tasty guacamole deviled egg are a simple, healthy hit!

Yields: 12 Servings

Total Time: 40 Minutes

Prep Time: 40 Minutes

Cook Time: 0 Minutes

Ingredients

- 2 ripe avocados
- 6 large hard-boiled eggs, peeled
- 1 tbsp. lime juice
- 1 tbsp. chopped chives
- ¼ cup chopped cilantro
- 1 tsp. red pepper flakes
- ½ tsp. sea salt
- Chili powder, for garnish

Directions

Cut the hard-boiled eggs into two equal parts and scoop out the yolks.

Mash together the egg yolks and avocados in a bowl until smooth. Stir in red pepper flakes, salt, lime juice, chives and cilantro; spoon the filling into the egg whites and refrigerate for at least 30 minutes.

Sprinkle with chili powder to serve.

Curried Roasted Cauliflower

What a healthy and tasty snack! It is simple, fast and very delicious.

Yield: 4 Servings

Total Time: 37 Minutes

Prep Time: 10 Minutes

Cook Time: 27 Minutes

Ingredients

- 1 large head cauliflower, trimmed and cut into small florets
- 1 cup coconut milk
- 2 tbsp. chopped fresh ginger root
- 2 tbsp. chopped onion
- 1 tbsp. extra virgin olive oil
- 2 tbsp. coconut oil
- 1 tsp. minced garlic
- ¼ tsp. mustard seeds
- ¼ tsp. ground cardamom
- ¼ tsp. ground cumin
- ¼ tsp. turmeric
- 1 tbsp. curry powder

Directions

Preheat your oven to 400°F. Prepare a 13x 18–inch pan by lining it with parchment paper.

Combine olive oil and coconut oil in a saucepan set over low heat; stir in garlic, ginger and onion and sauté for about 7 minutes or until onion is tender. Stir in coconut milk and simmer for about 5 minutes. Stir in cauliflower, mustard seeds, cardamom, cumin, turmeric, and curry; cook for about 15 minutes or until the liquid has reduced substantially.

Transfer the cauliflower mixture to the prepared pan and bake for about 30 minutes or until golden. Serve warm.

Healthy Spiced Nuts

These mild sweet and salty snacks are great to have on hand over holidays.

Yields: 4 Servings

Total Time: 20 Minutes

Prep Time: 10 Minutes

Cook Time: 10 Minutes

Ingredients

- 1 tbsp. extra virgin olive oil
- ⅔ cup walnuts
- ⅔ cup pecans
- ⅔ cup almonds
- ½ tsp. sea salt
- ½ tsp. pepper
- ½ tsp. cumin
- 1 tsp. chili powder

Directions

Put the nuts in a skillet set over medium heat and toast until lightly browned.

In the meantime, prepare the spice mixture; combine black pepper, cumin, chili and salt in a bowl.

Coat the toasted nuts with extra virgin olive oil and sprinkle with the spice mixture to serve.

Sesame Crackers

These are gluten free crackers that are made with protein-rich almond flour and sesame seeds. The recipe makes an amazingly crunchy gut-friendly snack.

Yields: 96 Crackers

Total Time: 32 Minutes

Prep Time: 20 Minutes

Cook Time: 12 Minutes

Ingredients

- 1 cup sesame seeds
- 2 tbsp. grapeseed oil
- 2 large free range eggs, beaten
- 1 ½ tsp. sea salt
- 3 cups almond flour, blanched

Directions

Stir together sesame seeds, almond flour, oil, eggs and salt in a large bowl until well combined.

Divide the dough into two portions.

Place each into two baking sheets lined with parchment papers and cover with parchment paper.

Spread the dough between the papers to cover the entire baking sheet and remove the top paper.

With a pizza cutter or knife, cut the dough into 2-inch squares and bake at 350°F until golden brown, for about 12 minutes.

Cool before serving.

MANAGE YOUR MICROBIOMES

Microbiome Diet Drinks

Fruity Kefir Smoothie
This fruity kefir smoothie makes for a perfect breakfast! It's fast, fun to make and packed with nutrition. This concoction is actually the best drink to start your morning off right!

Yields: 2 Servings

Total Time: 5 Minutes

Prep Time: 5 Minutes

Cook Time: 0 Minutes

Ingredients:

- 1 cup plain kefir
- Handful fresh spinach
- 1 navel orange, cut into segments
- 1/2 cup frozen blueberries
- 1/2 frozen banana

Directions:

Blend together all ingredients in a blender until very smooth. Enjoy!

Healthy Gut Smoothie

Cleanse your gut and restore your health with this amazingly tasty and healthy smoothie. It's a crowd pleaser!

Yields: 2 Servings

Total Time: 5 Minutes

Prep Time: 5 Minutes

Cook Time: 0 Minutes

Ingredients

- 2 tbsp. freshly squeezed lemon juice
- 1/2 clove garlic
- 2 green apples
- 3 carrots
- 1 inch of ginger

Directions

Blend together all ingredients until very smooth. Enjoy!

MANAGE YOUR MICROBIOMES

The Best Gut Health Smoothie

Are you suffering from digestive issues or disease? This intelligently crafted smoothie is your answer to your problem. It's very healthy.

Yields: 1 to 2 Servings

Total Time: 5 Minutes

Prep Time: 5 Minutes

Cook Time: 0 Minutes

Ingredients

- 1 ounce aloe vera juice
- ½ cup dairy free kefir
- ½ cup unsweetened almond milk
- 1 cup spinach
- 1 tsp. cinnamon
- 1 tsp. vanilla extract

Directions

Blend all ingredients until very smooth and creamy. Enjoy!

MANAGE YOUR MICROBIOMES

Berry & Flax Smoothie

This is a smart way to slip the healthy flax seeds and spinach into your diet. The smoothie is super healthy and very satisfying and you'll benefit from antioxidants (berries), probiotics (yogurt) and omega 3 and fiber (flax seeds) as well as the many benefits of spinach.

Yields: 1 to 2 Servings

Total Time: 5 Minutes

Prep Time: 5 Minutes

Cook Time: 0 Minutes

Ingredients

- 1 ½ cups yogurt
- 1 tsp. peeled ginger root
- 1 tbsp. flax seeds, ground
- 1 cup spinach
- ½ cup fresh berries

Directions

Blend and enjoy!

Happy Gut Energy Smoothie

Wow! This is a superb smoothie right here. It's packed with protein and fall-inspired flavors like cinnamon.

Yields: 2 Servings

Total Time: 5 Minutes

Prep Time: 5 Minutes

Cook Time: 0 Minutes

Ingredients

- 1 tsp. Probiotic Powder
- 1 big handful fresh spinach
- 8 oz. coconut water
- 1 tbsp. coconut oil
- 1 tbsp. chia seeds
- 2 drops vanilla
- A pinch cinnamon
- A few ice cubes

Directions

Blend and enjoy!

MANAGE YOUR MICROBIOMES

Chia Pineapple Colada Kefir

Quick and easy to make, this healthy drink is packed with probiotics, good for your gut.

Yields: 2 Servings

Total Time: 5 Minutes

Prep Time: 5 Minutes

Cook Time: 0 Minutes

Ingredients:

- 2 tsp. chia seeds
- 1/2 cup plain kefir
- 1/2 cup light coconut milk
- 1 cup diced fresh pineapple

Directions

Blend and enjoy!

Mango Green Tea

Kick start you day with this healthy drink. It will quench your thirst for caffeine along with prebiotic-rich yogurt and nutrient-dense mango.

Yields: 2 Servings

Total Time: 5 Minutes

Prep Time: 5 Minutes

Cook Time: 0 Minutes

Ingredients:

- 2 tbsp. vanilla protein powder
- 1/2 cup nonfat plain Greek yogurt
- 1 cup brewed green tea, chilled
- 1 cup frozen mango, diced

Directions

Blend together all ingredients and enjoy!

Tasty Stomach Healing Juice

If your stomach has been acting up, the digestion aiding superfood ingredients used in this juice might help. Loaded with healthy juices and ginger root, this juice provides an excellent way to ease your body into the day.

Ingredients

- 2 inch ginger root
- 2 oz. fennel juice
- 8 oz. celery juice
- 1 oz. aloe vera juice
- 1 oz. parsley juice
- 1 clove juiced garlic
- 3 oz. cabbage juice

Directions

Blend and enjoy!

Manage Your Microbiomes

Gut Cleansing Juice

Whether you indulged a lot at dinner or just want to load on nutrients, this wholesome, healthy smoothie –made with carrots, beets, kale, and a handful of dandelion – is just what the doctor ordered.

Ingredients

- 4 kale leaves
- 2.5 inch ginger root
- ½ red beet
- 4 Beet greens
- 4 Carrots
- A handful Dandelion leaves

Directions

Blend and enjoy!

Gut Healing Coconut Water Kefir Delight

Naturally high-fiber, low calorie cherries disguise the taste of lettuce in this delicious drink. It's superbly delicious and healthy!

Yields: 2 Servings

Total Time: 5 Minutes

Prep Time: 5 Minutes

Cook Time: 0 Minutes

Ingredients

- 2 cups purified water
- 2 cups organic lettuce leaves, rinsed, patted dry
- 1 small avocado, peeled, pitted
- 4 pitted dates, soaked for 20 minutes
- 1 peeled orange, seeds removed
- 2 cups frozen pitted dark cherries
- ½ tsp. turmeric
- Black pepper
- 1 cup cinnamon coconut water kefir

Directions

Blend everything until very smooth and creamy. Enjoy!

Almond Butter Chocolate Smoothie

This tasty smoothie has the flavors of a sweet smoothie without calories. Almond milk and butter adds extra proteins and the banana provides a potassium punch. You can have as a bedtime snack after dinner or an afternoon pick-me-up snack.

Yields: 1 Glass

Total Time: 5 Minutes

Prep Time: 5 Minutes

Cook Time: 0 Minutes

Ingredients

- 1 Banana
- 1 tbsp. cocoa powder
- 1 cup almond milk, unsweetened
- 1/3 cup almond butter
- 1 cup Ice

Directions

Blend all ingredients together until very smooth. Enjoy!

MANAGE YOUR MICROBIOMES

Delicious Strawberry Punch

This delicious drink is the perfect to make for a crowd. It's packed with healthy ingredients and very refreshing.

Yields: 16 Servings

Total Time: 5 Minutes

Prep Time: 5 Minutes

Cook Time: 0 Minutes

Ingredients:

- 32 ounces diet ginger ale
- 32 ounces fresh pineapple juice
- 1 cup fresh strawberries

Directions:

Blend the strawberries until smooth. Add ginger ale and pineapple juice and chill for at least 24 hours. Garnish with lime or lemon wedges, if desired.

Citrus Punch

This is a refreshing after lunch drink that everyone will love. It's good for your system too!

Yields: 12 Servings

Total Time: 5 Minutes

Prep Time: 5 Minutes

Cook Time: 0 Minutes

Ingredients:

- 1 cup fresh chopped pineapple
- 1/2 cup freshly squeezed lemon juice
- 4 cups water
- 6 ounces limeade, frozen

Directions:

In a food processor, puree fresh pineapple.

Combine the pureed pineapple with the remaining ingredients and chill for at least 1 hour.

Healthy Smoothie

Yields: 1 Serving

Total Time: 5 Minutes

Prep Time: 5 Minutes

Cook Time: 0 Minutes

Ingredients:

- 1 ripe banana
- 1/4 cantaloupe, with skin
- 1 peeled kiwi fruit

Directions:

Juice cantaloupe and kiwi fruit.

Combine the juice and banana in a blender and blend until smooth.

Gingery Grape Juice

Full of grape and gingery goodness, this drink is very refreshing especially when taken after lunch during those hot summer afternoons.

Yields: 1 Serving

Total Time: 5 Minutes

Prep Time: 5 Minutes

Cook Time: 0 Minutes

Ingredients:

- 2 cups red grapes
- 1 2-inch peeled ginger
- 1 medium lemon, peeled
- 4 oz. water

Directions:

Juice the lemon and combine with the remaining ingredients in a blender; blend until very smooth. Enjoy!

MANAGE YOUR MICROBIOMES

Detox Blend

Beets give this drink a rich red color while apple and lemon lend a great delicious flavor. The result is a beverage bursting with healthy ingredients while tasting like a sweet dessert.

Yields: 2 Servings

Total Time: 5 Minutes

Prep Time: 5 Minutes

Cook Time: 0 Minutes

Ingredients

- 5 carrots
- 4 celery stalks
- 1 small cucumber
- 1 beet
- 1 small apple
- 1/2 lemon

Directions

Juice everything together. Enjoy!

Fat-Burner Detox Juice

You'll never go wrong with this fat-burner detox juice. It's rich in essential nutrients and very energizing.

Yields: 2 Servings

Total Time: 5 Minutes

Prep Time: 5 Minutes

Cook Time: 0 Minutes

Ingredients

- 1 cup of choice greens
- 2 celery stalks
- 2 green apples
- 2 carrots
- 1 red sweet pepper
- 1 peeled lemon
- 1 ginger

Directions

Juice everything together. Enjoy!

Excellent Detoxifier

This beverage is great for detoxifying your entire system. You'll never get enough of it –it's tasty!

Yields: 4 Servings

Total Time: 5 Minutes

Prep Time: 5 Minutes

Cook Time: 0 Minutes

Ingredients

- ½ small green cabbage
- 3 or 4 celery stalks
- 3 or 4 carrots
- ½ bunch cilantro
- 1 whole lemon
- 1 small beet with greens
- Fennel tops from large bulb
- 1" chunk of fresh ginger root

Directions

Juice everything together. Enjoy!

Garlicky Green Juice

The gut friendly superfood, garlic, adds a unique flavor to this juice making it a great mid-afternoon drink.

Yields: 2 Servings

Total Time: 5 Minutes

Prep Time: 5 Minutes

Cook Time: 0 Minutes

Ingredients

- 1 green apple
- 1 cup kale
- 1 celery stalk
- 1 clove garlic
- Ginger

Directions

Juice everything together. Enjoy!

Brighten-Up Juice

Satisfy your vitamin A needs in one meal with this delicious green juice. The juice is healthy thanks to apples, carrots and spinach. Perfect for an AM start.

Yields: 1 Serving

Total Time: 5 Minutes

Prep Time: 5 Minutes

Cook Time: 0 Minutes

Ingredients

- 1/2 apple
- 4 carrots
- Handful of parsley
- Handful of spinach

Directions

Juice everything together. Enjoy!

The Super-8 Detox Juice

This delicious juice is chocked-full of superfoods. It's two times the flavor and nutrition!

Yields: 2 Servings

Total Time: 5 Minutes

Prep Time: 5 Minutes

Cook Time: 0 Minutes

Ingredients

- 1 collard leaf
- 1 kale leaf
- 1 broccoli floret
- 1 tomato
- 1/2 red pepper
- 1 carrot
- 1 stalk of celery
- Handful of parsley

Directions

Juice all ingredients and enjoy!

Tropical Dream

A swig of this vitamin-dense drink fuels your body. It's refreshing and good-for-you too!

Yields: 1 Serving

Total Time: 5 Minutes

Prep Time: 5 Minutes

Cook Time: 0 Minutes

Ingredients

- 14 Carrots
- 1/2 Papaya

Directions

Blend together all ingredients until smooth. Serve chilled.

Skin Soother Juice

This green goodie sneaks in the goodness of iron, important for healthy blood cells as well as muscle function. It's delicious too!

Yields: 3 Servings

Total Time: 5 Minutes

Prep Time: 5 Minutes

Cook Time: 0 Minutes

Ingredients

- 1 cucumber
- 8 carrots
- 1/2 bunch spinach

Directions

Blend together all ingredients until smooth. Serve chilled.

MANAGE YOUR MICROBIOMES

Smooth Skin Juice

On a juice cleanse? Try out this amazingly refreshing and healthy juice. It's loaded with nutrients and it's very filling.

Yields: 2 Servings

Total Time: 5 Minutes

Prep Time: 5 Minutes

Cook Time: 0 Minutes

Ingredients

- 1 pear
- 2 Granny Smith green apples
- 1 large beet
- 1 handful dandelion greens
- 1 whole fennel bulb

Directions

Juice everything and combine. Serve chilled.

Berricious Smoothie

Packed with antioxidants (thanks, berries!), this tasty smoothie is a snap to make. You may want to add a drizzle of raw honey to sweeten.

Yields: 2 Servings

Total Time: 5 Minutes

Prep Time: 5 Minutes

Cook Time: 0 Minutes

Ingredients

- 1/8 cup rolled oats
- 1 cup purified water
- 1/2 cup coconut milk
- 1 1/2 cups mixed berries (blackberries, raspberries, blueberries)

Directions

Blend all ingredients together until smooth.

Cocoa Bliss

This is a creamy, probiotic rich drink that everyone in your household will love. It's healthy and super delicious.

Yields: 1 Servings

Total Time: 5 Minutes

Prep Time: 5 Minutes

Cook Time: 0 Minutes

Ingredients

- 1/2 cup strawberries
- 1/2 cup nonfat plain Greek yogurt
- 1 tbsp. dark cocoa powder
- 1 cup ice

Directions

Blend all ingredients together until smooth.

Lean Detox Smoothie

Start your morning with a sip of this smoothie and you'll be on your way to a bikini body. It's loaded with vitamins and essential minerals.

Yields: 1 Servings

Total Time: 5 Minutes

Prep Time: 5 Minutes

Cook Time: 0 Minutes

Ingredients

- 1/2 frozen peach
- 1 cup brewed green tea
- 1 scoop vanilla protein powder

Directions

Blend together all ingredients in a blender until smooth.

MANAGE YOUR MICROBIOMES

Super Detox Smoothie

Detoxify your body with this nutrient-dense smoothie. You can use coconut water in place of purified water for a tropical twist.

Yields: 1 Servings

Total Time: 5 Minutes

Prep Time: 5 Minutes

Cook Time: 0 Minutes

Ingredients

- 1 cup purified water
- 1/2 cup steamed broccoli
- 1/2 pear
- 1/2 carrot, peeled

Directions

Chop up everything and add to a blender; blend until smooth. Enjoy!

Gingery Pineapple Paradise

Reminiscent of ginger, this beverage is loaded with good-for-you ingredients like mango, apple and pineapple. You'll never believe how healthy and delicious this sweet treat it!

Yields: 2 Servings

Total Time: 5 Minutes

Prep Time: 5 Minutes

Cook Time: 0 Minutes

Ingredients

- 1-inch piece fresh ginger
- 1/2 a pineapple
- 1/2 a lime
- 1 apple
- 1/2 a ripe mango, peeled

Directions

Blend together all ingredients until smooth. Serve over ice.

MANAGE YOUR MICROBIOMES

Date Orange Smoothie

Start your day with a big boost of energy with this date orange smoothie. It is packed with healthy fruits, almond milk and coconut cream, which help revitalize your body. It's a crowd pleaser.

Yields: 1 Serving

Total Time: 5 Minutes

Prep Time: 5 Minutes

Cook Time: 0 Minutes

Ingredients

- 2 pitted dates
- Flesh of 1 large orange
- ¼-1/2 cup vanilla almond milk
- 2 tbsp. coconut cream

Directions

Blend together all ingredients until smooth.

MANAGE YOUR MICROBIOMES

The Super Cleanser

Start your morning by eliminating harmful toxins, restoring your system and resetting your system with this super cleanser drink. It's super healthy and very delicious.

Yields: 2 Servings

Total Time: 5 Minutes

Prep Time: 5 Minutes

Cook Time: 0 Minutes

Ingredients

- 2 tbsp. freshly squeezed lemon juice
- 2 tbsp. maple syrup
- Pinch of cayenne pepper

Directions

Combine lemon juice, cayenne pepper and maple syrup in a glass; stir in water until well combined. Enjoy!

MANAGE YOUR MICROBIOMES

Berry Magic Juice

Blueberries are rich antioxidant superfood good for your immune system ad brain function. This simple but superb juice can be tweaked to your liking, but remember to use only healthy ingredients.

Yields: 2 Servings

Total Time: 5 Minutes

Prep Time: 5 Minutes

Cook Time: 0 Minutes

Ingredients

- ¼ cup fresh cranberries
- ½ cup fresh blueberries
- 1 sweet apple
- 1 pear
- 6 strawberries

Directions

Juice berries, apple and pear into a glass. Stir to combine well. Enjoy!

Citrus Drink

Re-energize at lunchtime with this citrus drink. It's loaded with vitamins and antioxidants to keep your system going.

Yields: 2 Servings

Total Time: 5 Minutes

Prep Time: 5 Minutes

Cook Time: 0 Minutes

Ingredients

- 1 lemon
- 1 orange
- 1 large grapefruit

Directions

Juice red grapefruit and orange; set aside. Squeeze in the lemon juice and stir to combine well.

Strawberry Papaya Smoothie

Rich in antioxidants and fiber, papaya is a nutritious fruit! And blended with strawberries and kefir makes a great drink to keep your immune system and gut going strong, it makes for a perfect start to your morning.

Yields: 2 Servings

Total Time: 5 Minutes

Prep Time: 5 Minutes

Cook Time: 0 Minutes

Ingredients

- 1 cup coconut kefir
- 1 cup sliced papaya
- ½ cup strawberries
- ½ cup water and ice
- 1 scoop whey protein powder

Directions

Blend together all the ingredients. Enjoy!

Wonder Cleanser

Receive your daily dose of nutrients with this doctors-approved blend. If you feel like not getting adequate vitamins and other essential nutrients from your daily diet, this foolproof drink loads on a powerful antioxidant punch that will help boost your immune system.

Yields: 2 Servings

Total Time: 5 Minutes

Prep Time: 5 Minutes

Cook Time: 0 Minutes

Ingredients

- ¼ cup chopped watercress
- ½ cup arugula leaves
- ½ cup romaine leaves
- ½ cup spinach leaves
- 3 large carrots

Directions

Juice watercress, arugula leaves, romaine leaves and spinach separately; combine the juice in a pitcher. Juice carrots and stir into the pitcher. Enjoy!

Papaya & Pear Detox Juice

During flu and cold season, catching some type of bug can seem almost unavoidable. Fill up on this papaya and pear juice that will help you in getting the nutrients required to stay healthy.

Yields: 2 Servings

Total Time: 5 Minutes

Prep Time: 5 Minutes

Cook Time: 0 Minutes

Ingredients

- ¾ cup chopped papaya
- 1 sweet apple
- 2 pears
- 1 lemon

Directions

Juice apples, pears, and papaya separately and mix the juice in a pitcher. Squeeze in lemon juice and stir to combine well.

Mint & Cucumber Detox Juice

This juice is just a delicious drink. Take a sip to revitalize your energy level. And under 200 calories, this refreshing and tasty blend is a great way to start off your day.

Yields: 2 Servings

Total Time: 5 Minutes

Prep Time: 5 Minutes

Cook Time: 0 Minutes

Ingredients

- ½ cup diced pineapple
- 2 large cucumbers
- 1 cup chopped kale
- Ginger, ¼ inch, grated
- 1 tbsp. freshly squeezed lemon juice
- ¼ cup chopped green bell pepper
- ¼ cup chopped mint

Directions

Juice cucumber and pineapple and set aside in a pitcher. Juice ginger, kale, green bell pepper and mint; combine with cucumber and pineapple juice and stir in lemon juice. Enjoy!

Apple Cider Vinegar & Grape Juice

End your day strong with this nutritious dinner drink.

It has the ability to help you get rid of harmful toxins, restore your system and energize your body in just three days.

Yields: 2 Servings

Total Time: 5 Minutes

Prep Time: 5 Minutes

Cook Time: 0 Minutes

Ingredients

- ½ tsp. cinnamon powder
- 2 tbsp. apple cider vinegar
- 1 cup grapes

Directions

Juice grapes and pour into a glass; stir in cinnamon powder and apple cider vinegar. Enjoy!

Parting Shot...

Your body is astoundingly adept at adapting and making do with whatever you feed it. It has developed an uncanny ability to survive on even the strangest of diets and this is one of the greatest adaptations of mankind, a species that has evolved from days when food and water was a luxury to a place where food is available in every street corner.

Today bad food is cheap and plentiful – perhaps too much so.

If you want to be successful in your health and weight loss journey, you need to pay close attention to diversity of the food you choose to feed your microbiomes.

Health experts today consider microbiomes as an "organ". However, gut microbiomes are an "acquired" organ - gut colonization starts right after you are born and evolves as you grow. That said, you should feed your microbiomes well in order to stay well.

Cleansing your gut and sticking to a gut-friendly diet has been proven one of the most effective ways of losing weight and maintaining a healthy body. Take it one day at a time and you will soon see some fantastic results!

Don't be afraid to go through this guide again and again until all the information becomes second nature.

Nourish your microbiomes and live a healthy life.

INDEX

acidophilus, 36
Acne, 49
allergies, 49
almond flour, 59, 63, 159
almond milk, 61, 65, 163, 171, 190
almonds, 59, 61, 82, 83, 97, 101, 109, 158
aloe vera juice, 163, 168
antibiotics, 22, 23
anti-inflammatory, 21, 32
Anxiety, 49
appetite, 45
apple, 79, 94, 104, 108, 109, 113, 116, 131, 133, 142, 147, 176, 179, 180, 189, 192, 196, 198
apple cider vinegar, 79, 104, 108, 109, 113, 116, 131, 133, 142, 147, 198
apples, 94, 109, 162, 177, 180, 184, 196
artichokes, 17, 98
arugula, 92, 107, 195
asparagus, 40, 79, 89, 111, 112, 117, 118, 137
Asparagus, 5, 6, 18, 79, 89, 111, 117, 137
aspergillus oryzae, 26
Asthma, 49
Autism, 49
Autoimmune diseases, 49
avocado, 71, 84, 92, 103, 106, 127, 140, 170
bacillus subtilis, 37
bacon, 66
bacteria, 15, 16, 20, 22, 23, 28, 32, 35, 40, 42, 45, 46, 47, 48, 49, 51, 52, 54
bad cholesterol, 32
Baechu, 24
baking powder, 72, 76, 83
baking soda, 72, 76
baking-powder, 82
balsamic vinegar, 151, 153
banana, 41, 161, 171, 174
barley, 26
basil, 68, 85, 125, 133, 134, 145
beef, 54, 119, 127
beer, 88
beet, 104, 169, 176, 178, 184
beets, 104, 151, 169
berries, 61, 65, 71, 101, 164, 185, 192
beverage, 31, 33, 71, 176, 178, 189
Bifidobacterium lactis, 39
black tea, 33
blood glucose, 32
blood pressure, 32
blood stream, 45
blueberries, 65, 161, 185, 192
body, 9, 12, 22, 23, 32, 33, 39, 42, 45, 48, 52, 53, 54, 115, 168, 182, 187, 188, 190, 198, 199
broccoli, 63, 64, 181, 188
brown rice, 26, 134
buckwheat flour, 76
butter, 26, 72, 171
butternut squash, 148
cabbage, 24, 25, 30, 94, 100, 114, 115, 123, 131, 168, 178

MANAGE YOUR MICROBIOMES

calcium, 22, 23, 25, 35, 40
calories, 17, 44, 92, 171, 197
cancer, 22, 40, 42, 51
Cancer, 49
candida, 23
candidiasis, 22, 23
cantaloupe, 174
capers, 78, 98
cardamom, 156
carrot, 24, 25, 94, 128, 150, 181, 188
carrots, 18, 87, 94, 100, 114, 121, 131, 150, 154, 162, 169, 176, 177, 178, 180, 183, 195
Carrots, 17, 169, 182
cauliflower, 115, 128, 156, 157
celery, 87, 97, 103, 115, 127, 138, 143, 154, 168, 176, 177, 178, 179, 181
Celery, 6, 143
cells, 9, 48, 51, 183
cheese, 53, 65, 69, 70, 74, 75, 79, 80, 81, 90, 95, 98, 117, 118, 143
cherries, 170
chicken, 53, 54, 87, 92, 97, 100, 109, 121, 124, 125, 129, 130, 131, 132, 133, 134
chickpeas, 103, 113
chicory, 40
chicory root, 40
chile powder, 116
chili pepper, 24
chili powder, 116, 121, 122, 127, 155, 158
Chili powder, 155
Chinese cabbages, 24
chips, 53, 139, 147

chives, 58, 85, 125, 135, 155
chocolate, 46, 53, 72
chromium, 22
chronic illnesses, 9, 13, 42, 45, 48
chronic inflammation, 22
cilantro, 94, 110, 138, 155, 178
cinnamon, 59, 61, 65, 71, 82, 83, 141, 163, 165, 170, 198
cocoa powder, 171, 186
coconut, 59, 63, 66, 68, 71, 72, 76, 82, 83, 84, 85, 93, 115, 117, 118, 128, 132, 141, 156, 165, 166, 170, 185, 188, 190, 194
coconut flour, 72, 82, 83
coconut milk, 71, 82, 83, 85, 115, 117, 156, 166, 185
coconut oil, 59, 63, 66, 68, 72, 76, 82, 83, 85, 93, 117, 118, 128, 132, 141, 156, 165
Coconut oil, 58
coconut water, 84, 165, 170, 188
collard, 181
colon, 22, 39, 40
colon cancer, 40
condiment, 24
conscious food choices, 12
constipation, 23, 30
cookies, 46, 53
copper, 26
coriander, 110
courgette, 95
cow, 31
cranberries, 59, 97, 109, 192
cucumber, 84, 86, 90, 106, 107, 138, 176, 183, 197

cucumbers, 24, 86, 107, 116, 197
cumin, 106, 110, 121, 122, 127, 156, 158
currants, 149
curry powder, 97, 156
dandelion, 40, 169, 184
Dandelion, 169
dates, 33, 59, 170, 190
dementia, 51
Dental cavities, 49
Depression, 49
diabetes, 13, 22, 42, 45, 92
Diabetes, 49
diarrhea, 23, 30, 49
diet, 9, 13, 22, 23, 39, 40, 42, 44, 45, 46, 47, 48, 51, 52, 53, 54, 89, 131, 164, 172, 195, 199
Diet, 4, 5, 6, 9, 10, 42, 44, 48, 51, 52, 111, 136, 161
dietary fiber., 15
digestion, 15, 46, 168
digestive disorders, 23
digestive enzymes, 15, 19, 30
digestive system, 12, 48, 49
Dijon mustard, 88, 91, 105, 111
dill, 58, 62, 85, 86, 103
doctor, 50, 169
dysbiosis, 51
eating disorders, 51
ecosystem, 45, 51
Eczema, 49
egg whites, 78, 117, 118, 132, 155
egg yolk, 62, 118
egg yolks, 117, 118, 155
eggplant, 125

eggplants, 24
eggs, 42, 56, 58, 62, 63, 64, 66, 68, 69, 70, 72, 73, 74, 75, 76, 79, 80, 82, 83, 85, 95, 128, 140, 149, 155, 159
endotoxins, 44, 45
energy, 9, 10, 45, 190, 197
extra virgin olive oil, 56, 62, 69, 80, 86, 88, 89, 91, 94, 95, 101, 105, 107, 108, 109, 110, 111, 112, 113, 114, 115, 119, 121, 123, 124, 125, 129, 131, 133, 134, 135, 136, 137, 139, 145, 146, 147, 148, 150, 151, 152, 153, 156, 158
Fat, 4, 7, 44, 177
fennel, 86, 168, 184
fermented beverages, 22
fermented foods, 23
figs, 153
fish, 24, 33, 54, 110, 116, 120, 134
flavonoids, 15
flora, 39, 45, 49
flu, 49, 87, 196
Food, 4, 9, 40, 46, 48
food choices, 13
fructo-oligosaccharides, 39
fruit, 12, 54, 105, 174, 194
fungi, 48, 51
fungus, 26
garlic, 24, 25, 40, 56, 58, 62, 74, 75, 80, 85, 88, 91, 103, 104, 105, 110, 113, 115, 116, 121, 123, 128, 131, 133, 138, 143, 145, 149, 156, 162, 168, 179
Garlic, 5, 6, 19, 88, 113, 123
Gastric ulcer, 49

genes, 10
Genghis Khan, 31
GI –bifidobacteria, 39
ginger, 13, 24, 25, 110, 116, 156, 162, 164, 168, 169, 172, 175, 177, 178, 189, 197
goat's, 31, 36
grapefruit, 105, 108, 193
grapefruit juice, 105
grapes, 175, 198
grapeseed oil, 148, 149, 159
green beans, 142
green tea, 13, 54, 167, 187
greens, 40, 85, 109, 169, 177, 178, 184
gut bacteria, 13, 15, 19, 21, 22, 39
halitosis, 22
health, 9, 10, 12, 13, 15, 22, 31, 35, 39, 40, 42, 49, 50, 51, 52, 54, 140, 162, 199
heart disease, 22, 45
Hippocrates, 12, 48
honey, 72, 82, 83, 101, 105, 142, 152
hormones, 10, 46
hot pepper, 24
hot pepper flakes, 24
hunter, 53
hypothalamus, 45
IBS, 23
Ice, 171
ice cubes, 84, 165
illness, 12, 51
immune, 22, 23, 25, 35, 51, 192, 194, 195
inflammation, 45, 49, 51
inflammatory bowel disease, 40

intestinal tract, 16
intestines, 10, 39
inulin, 17, 18, 20, 39
inulins, 39
Jerusalem, 16, 17, 40
Jerusalem artichokes, 17
Jerusalem Artichokes, 16
jicama, 94
Jicama, 5, 19, 94
joint pains, 44
junk food, 47, 54
kalamata olives, 90, 98, 129, 153
kale, 71, 100, 106, 108, 125, 126, 139, 146, 147, 169, 179, 181, 197
kefir, 31, 32, 72, 73, 74, 75, 76, 161, 163, 166, 170, 194
kefiran, 32
kimchi, 24, 25, 30, 116
Kimchi, 5, 23, 24, 25, 116
kiwi, 174
Kombucha, 33, 34
lactobacillus, 25, 32, 36, 39
lactose intolerance, 22, 35
lactose intolerant, 31
leaky gut syndrome, 44
leek, 40, 81, 95
leeks, 24, 40, 80, 115
Leeks, 15
lemon, 84, 86, 90, 91, 98, 103, 107, 111, 112, 114, 124, 131, 135, 137, 162, 172, 173, 175, 176, 177, 178, 191, 193, 196, 197
lime, 94, 106, 108, 110, 138, 155, 172, 189
lime juice, 94, 106, 108, 110, 155

limeade, 173
liver, 119
Malnutrition, 49
manganese, 15, 26
mango, 92, 167, 189
maple syrup, 191
mayonnaise, 97
measles, 49
meat, 12, 28, 42, 53, 54, 74, 110, 121, 124, 131, 134
metabolism, 10
Michael Kearney, 38
microbes, 10, 44, 46, 47, 49, 52
microbiome, 4, 9, 10, 11, 12, 13, 15, 19, 20, 21, 42, 44, 45, 46, 47, 48, 49, 50, 51, 52, 53, 54, 56, 71, 74, 111
Microbiome, 4, 5, 6, 10, 44, 48, 51, 52, 56, 86, 111, 136, 161
microbiome diet, 9, 10, 11, 12, 13, 44, 45, 48, 49, 50, 53, 54
microorganisms, 39
minerals, 22, 42, 48, 82, 187
mint, 135, 197
Miso, 26, 27
Mongol Empire, 31
muffin, 72, 78
mushrooms, 56, 74, 75, 100, 145
mussels, 88
natto, 37, 38
Natto, 37
nattokinase, 38
natural, 13, 17, 18, 21, 42, 45, 47, 53
neurons, 46
neurotransmitters, 46
non-GMO products, 27

nutmeg, 74, 75, 115, 117, 118, 137
Nutmeg, 115
nutrients, 10, 12, 13, 18, 26, 48, 154, 169, 177, 184, 195, 196
nutrition, 9, 12, 39, 42, 48, 90, 161, 181
nutritional value, 44
nutritional yeast, 139
nutritionist, 50
nutritious food, 12, 54
nuts, 42, 53, 54, 81, 143, 145, 149, 152, 158
oats, 185
obese, 44, 45
obesity, 13, 44, 45, 51
Obesity, 50
oligofructose, 39
oligosporus, 28
omega 3 fatty acids, 46
onion, 24, 25, 40, 66, 69, 74, 75, 78, 85, 86, 87, 90, 92, 95, 98, 100, 101, 103, 104, 105, 106, 110, 121, 127, 128, 129, 133, 134, 138, 146, 156
onions, 40, 67, 69, 76, 85, 119, 121, 122, 133, 142
orange, 82, 83, 94, 105, 161, 170, 190, 193
orange juice, 82, 83, 94
orange zest, 82
oregano, 90, 91, 100, 121, 122, 129, 134
organ, 12, 48, 199
organic, 14, 27, 45, 62, 69, 79, 80, 82, 84, 85, 100, 170
overweight, 44, 45
Papaya, 7, 182, 194, 196

paprika, 101, 125, 134
parasites, 51
parsley, 72, 80, 84, 85, 93, 104, 129, 168, 180, 181
parsnip, 115
pathogens, 33, 48
peach, 187
pear, 94, 97, 184, 188, 192, 196
pears, 196
pecans, 59, 61, 158
pepper, 25, 56, 58, 62, 66, 68, 69, 70, 74, 79, 80, 86, 88, 89, 90, 91, 92, 93, 94, 95, 98, 100, 103, 104, 105, 106, 111, 112, 113, 115, 117, 118, 121, 122, 123, 124, 125, 127, 128, 129, 131, 134, 135, 137, 142, 154, 155, 158, 170, 177, 181, 191, 197
peppercorns, 87
pesto, 120, 145
pineapple, 166, 172, 173, 189, 197
plant based diet, 42, 47, 53
plantains, 141
plums, 82, 83
pneumonia, 28
prebiotic, 17, 39, 40, 167
prebiotics, 18, 19, 39, 40
probiotic foods, 22, 23, 24, 26, 35, 37
Probiotic Foods, 4, 22, 23
Probiotic Powder, 165
probiotics, 13, 22, 23, 36, 39, 40, 46, 164, 166
processed foods, 13, 42, 44, 53
protein, 26, 32, 35, 37, 42, 78, 159, 165, 167, 187, 194

protozoa, 48
psoriasis, 51
puberty, 44
Qin Shi Huangdi, 31
quinoa, 93, 106, 120
radish, 24, 94
Radishes, 15
rapeseed oil, 65
raspberries, 65, 185
raw honey, 72, 101, 185
recipe, 21, 58, 59, 61, 65, 66, 69, 74, 89, 90, 92, 95, 103, 106, 109, 114, 120, 127, 128, 131, 133, 135, 137, 145, 159
recipes, 9, 11, 32, 35, 54, 65
red pepper flakes, 58, 62, 113, 121, 122, 155
red wine vinegar, 91
romaine lettuce, 90, 114
roots, 53
rosemary, 89, 115
sage, 72, 100, 124
salads, 28, 33, 90, 97
salmon, 62, 78, 89, 134
salt, 24, 26, 30, 56, 62, 63, 66, 68, 69, 70, 72, 74, 76, 78, 79, 80, 85, 86, 87, 88, 89, 90, 91, 92, 93, 94, 95, 100, 103, 104, 105, 106, 107, 108, 109, 111, 112, 113, 114, 115, 116, 117, 118, 121, 123, 124, 125, 127, 128, 129, 131, 132, 134, 135, 136, 137, 138, 139, 142, 145, 146, 147, 148, 149, 150, 151, 152, 155, 158, 159
Salt, 6, 58, 62, 90, 100, 103, 106, 119, 128, 136, 142, 147
sauce, 24, 37, 83, 110, 116, 140

sauerkraut, 12, 30, 31
Sauerkraut, 30
sausage, 63, 64, 74, 75
scallions, 116
scurvy, 12
seasoning, 26
seaweed, 26
seeds, 42, 53, 59, 82, 83, 101, 105, 143, 148, 156, 159, 164, 165, 166, 170
sepsis, 28
serum cholesterol, 35
shallot, 88
sheep, 31, 65, 69, 74, 79, 80, 90, 95, 98
shrimp, 110, 128
smoothie, 54, 84, 161, 162, 163, 164, 165, 169, 171, 185, 187, 188, 190
smoothies, 32, 35
snacks, 26, 139, 141, 158
sodium, 44
soy bean, 26
soy beans, 28, 42
Soy sauce, 27
soybean, 37
spice, 21, 59, 82, 83, 134, 142, 158
spinach, 56, 69, 70, 74, 75, 80, 81, 84, 95, 101, 104, 105, 106, 125, 126, 131, 149, 161, 163, 164, 165, 180, 183, 195
sprouts, 97
starches, 46
stomach, 45, 48, 54, 168
strawberries, 65, 101, 172, 186, 192, 194
sugar, 44, 46

superfoods, 15, 21, 181
supplements, 22, 39
synthesis, 20, 23
tahini dressing, 114
tamari, 27
tapioca flour, 72
tarragon, 69, 80, 88
tempeh, 28
Tempeh, 28, 29
thyme, 72, 74, 75, 88, 93, 113, 115, 131, 134, 153
tilapia, 120, 134
tofu, 26
tomato, 68, 78, 90, 98, 100, 121, 122, 127, 129, 130, 133, 181
tomatoes, 56, 58, 104, 106, 110, 121, 122, 125, 127, 133
tooth decay, 44
turmeric, 110, 156, 157, 170
Turmeric, 20
vaginitis, 23
vanilla extract, 71, 76, 163
Vegetable, 4, 56
vegetable broth, 113
vegetables, 12, 13, 17, 24, 28
vegetarian, 28, 42, 54
viruses, 48, 49, 51
vitamin, 15, 23, 26, 28, 30, 35, 37, 114, 180, 182
vitamin A, 15, 114, 180
walnuts, 145, 158
watercress, 195
weight loss, 9, 10, 11, 42, 199
wheat bran, 40
white vinegar, 101
white-wine vinegar, 105
whole foods, 12

Worcestershire sauce, **101**
yeast infections, **23**, **35**
yogurt, **13**, **23**, **35**, **36**, **97**, **164**, **167**, **186**

Yogurt, **35**, **36**
zinc, **26**
zucchini, **69**, **85**, **135**, **142**